Liturgy and Literature

By the Same Author

Charlemagne's Cousins (1967)
Son of Charlemagne (1961)
Early Medieval Theology (with George E. McCracken,
    1957)
Amalarius of Metz (1954)
Agobard of Lyons: Churchman and Critic (1953)
A History of the University of Mississippi (1949)
Life and Thought of a Country Preacher (1942)

Liturgy and Literature

Selected Essays

By ALLEN CABANISS

UNIVERSITY OF ALABAMA PRESS

University, Alabama

Table of Contents

Acknowledgments 7

Introduction 11

1. The Worship of "Most Primitive" Christianity 21
2. Early Christian Nighttime Worship 30
3. A Fresh Exegesis of Mark 2:1–12 37
4. A Note on the Liturgy of the Apocalypse 42
5. Wisdom 18:14–15: An Early Christmas Text 53
6. Christmas Echoes at Paschaltide 58
7. The Harrowing of Hell, Psalm 24, and Pliny the Younger: A Note 62
8. Petronius and the Gospel before the Gospels? 72
   a. A Footnote to the 'Petronian Question' 72
   b. The *Satiricon* and the Christian Oral Tradition 77
   c. The Matron of Ephesus Again: An Analysis 81
   d. The Matron of Ephesus: An Identification 93
9. A Note on the Date of the Great Advent Antiphons 97
10. *Beowulf* and the Liturgy 101
11. Joseph of Arimathea and a Chalice 109
12. Alleluia: A Word and Its Effect 114
13. Shakespeare and the Holy Rosary 122
    Epilogue 133
    Notes 136
    Index 173

Acknowledgments

I am indebted to the Department of History of the University of Mississippi, Professor John Hebron Moore, Chairman, for a small subvention to assist publication of this book. As always, my sister, Frances C. Stephens, has helped in reading proof.

And I want to express my thanks to the editors, publishers, and copyright owners of the various journals who have allowed me to reprint, with some modifications, the essays.

"The Worship of 'Most Primitive' Christianity," reprinted by permission of the American Academy of Religion, copyright owner, from *The Journal of Bible and Religion*, 26, no. 4 (October, 1958), pp. 318–21.

"Early Christian Nighttime Worship," reprinted by permission of the American Academy of Religion, copyright owner, from *The Journal of Bible and Religion*, 25, no. 1 (January, 1957), pp. 30–33.

"A Fresh Exegesis of Mark 2:1–12," reprinted by permission, from *Interpretation*, 11, no. 3 (July, 1957), pp. 324–27.

"A Note on the Liturgy of the Apocalypse," reprinted by permission, from *Interpretation*, 7, no. 1 (January, 1953), pp. 78–86.

"Wisdom 18:14–15: An Early Christmas Text," reprinted by permission, from *Vigiliae Christianae*, 10, no. 2 (July, 1956), pp. 97–102.

"Christmas Echoes at Paschaltide," reprinted by permission, from *New Testament Studies*, 9, no. 1 (October, 1962), pp. 67–69.

"The Harrowing of Hell, Psalm 24, and Pliny the Younger: A Note," reprinted by permission, from *Vigiliae Christianae*, 7, no. 2 (April, 1953), pp. 65–74.

"A Footnote to the 'Petronian Question,' " reprinted by permission of the University of Chicago Press, from *Classical Philology*, 49, no. 2 (April, 1954), pp. 98–102.

"The *Satiricon* and the Christian Oral Tradition," reprinted by permission, from *Greek, Roman, and Byzantine Studies*, 3, no. 1 (Winter, 1960), pp. 36–39.

"The Matron of Ephesus Again: An Analysis," reprinted by permission, from *Studies in English*, 2 (1961), pp. 41–53.

"The Matron of Ephesus: An Identification," reprinted by permission, from *Studies in English*, 3 (1962), pp. 75–77.

"A Note on the Date of the Great Advent Antiphons," reprinted by permission, from *Speculum*, 22, no. 3 (July, 1947), pp. 440–42.

"*Beowulf* and the Liturgy," reprinted by permission, from *The Journal of English and Germanic Philology*, 54, no. 2 (April, 1955), pp. 195–201. This paper has also been reprinted in Lewis E. Nicholson, ed., *An Anthology of Beowulf Criticism* (Notre Dame, Ind.: University of Notre Dame Press, 1963), pp. 223–32.

"Joseph of Arimathea and a Chalice," reprinted by permission, from *Studies in English*, 4 (1963), pp. 61–67.

"Alleluia: A Word and Its Effect," reprinted by permission, from *Studies in English*, 5 (1964), pp. 67–74.

"Shakespeare and the Holy Rosary," reprinted by permission, from *Studies in English*, 1 (1960), pp. 118–28.

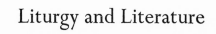

Liturgy and Literature

Introduction

It is coming to be recognized that Christianity was, from its inception, a liturgical religion—that it has always worshiped in an orderly and ceremonious manner. Far from being "round, unvarnished," and plain, the Christian cultus was rich, colorful, beautiful, and deeply moving, as may be demonstrated by referring to four sources of evidence.

First, it is known that Christ, the apostles, and early disciples were very familiar with the Temple on Mount Zion and continued to participate in its liturgy, resorting thither to worship,[1] keeping the hours of the daily service.[2] According to ancient tradition, Saint James the Just, foster-brother of Jesus and first bishop of Jerusalem, prayed in the Temple so habitually that his knees became as hardened as those of a camel.[3] Saint John the Evangelist is reputed to have worn the breastplate of a Jewish priest.[4] Saint Paul was so deeply colored in mind and thought by Temple ceremonial that he often interchanged the language of Temple and church.[5]

The Temple with which earliest Christians were acquainted was the one erected by Zerubbabel after the Babylonian captivity, greatly expanded and lavishly adorned by
Herod. Behind that Temple was the structure by Solomon,
described with precise detail in I Kings 6–8 and II Chron-
icles 3–7. Further in the background was the Mosaic tabernacle, long since crumbled into the dust of Palestine, but
continuing to exercise a peculiar fascination upon affections
of pious Jews and Christians alike.[6]

Worship in the Temple was a series of highly developed,
awe-inspiring, and dramatic liturgical services. The Psalter
was perhaps arranged as it is today to serve as a hymnal for
the Temple restored by Zerubbabel. Indeed several modern
editions indicate the particular liturgical function of many
of the Psalms.[7] Gentile converts who had never participated
in Temple worship would be quite familiar with it from
study of the Bible. Virtually the entire book of Leviticus,
for example, is devoted to a meticulous description of it.
Colors, music, incense, ceremonial vestments, and artistic
imagery were there, exerting incalculable, even if intangible,
influence on primitive Christianity.

A *second* factor operative on the earliest Christians was a
prophetic vision of worship coming to them especially in the
writings of Ezekiel.[8] Here the Temple and its liturgy were
given an ethereal quality of worship-as-it-should-be.[9] In the
last two chapters of the Revelation, the author's portrayal of
a New Jerusalem is reminiscent of Ezekiel's ideal Temple
and its environs. Another prophet, Isaiah, "saw" the worship of God in heaven and gave the church a hymn, the
Sanctus, which it has continued using to this day.[10] As now
sung, that hymn is indeed prefaced by a declaration that
earthly worship is in some way related to—is continuous
with—angelic worship in heaven. In the epistle to the He-

brews there are express statements that in heaven Christ performs the perfect service, of which earthly liturgy is a faint representation.[11] So we have as it were a *third* factor emerging from the second and closely related to it, the concept of a glorious celestial liturgy to be imitated by the church here on earth.

For twenty-five to fifty years or more after the death of Christ, the church was prevailingly Semitic, made up of people whose worship was formed by the Jewish matrix from which they came. But we should not discount the trickle of converts from Mediterranean heathenism, due to become in time a majority element in Christianity. Many early Christians had formerly satisfied their longings in the religions of Mithras, Isis and Osiris, the Magna Mater, and other Oriental cults.[12] Quite naturally, they brought with them alien ideas that inevitably impinged upon Christianity, and some of the rites of those religions may have affected Christian worship.[13] And so there is a *fourth*, a pagan, factor to be noted, which had already in a degree penetrated pre-Christian Judaism.

Saint Ignatius of Antioch suggests a definite coloring when he speaks of the Eucharist in terms reflecting a pagan sacrificial meal in which the worshipers mystically "ate" their god.[14] Saint Justin Martyr felt it necessary, in his *Apology* addressed to Emperor Antoninus Pius, to defend the Eucharist from charges that it was an imitation of Mithraic ceremonies.[15] From such a statement it is legitimate also to deduce that Christian worship was somehow comparable to the pomp of a pagan service. Some of the language of Saint Paul's letters indicate that influence.[16] A vivid passage, to which no English translation can do justice without periphrasis, is a luminous revelation of such impact. "That I may be for the heathen a *leitourgos* (liturgical ministrant)

of Messiah Jesus," he says, "*hierourgounta* (serving in priest-
ly manner) the gospel of God, so that the *prosphora* (sacrificial oblation), namely, the heathen, may be acceptable
when it has been *hegiasmene* (ritually purified) by the Holy
Spirit." [17]

Original readers and hearers of that verse came chiefly
from Hebraic tradition, but some were surely converts from
various Mediterranean cults. Those words, so redolent of
both pagan and Jewish sacrificial systems, would therefore
conjure up a mental image of Saint Paul, clad in the ornate
vesture of a priest, heathen or Aaronic, standing beside an
altar amid billowing clouds of incense, ready with liturgical
words and stately movements to offer up a holocaust to
Deity. It is a very daring metaphor, either amazingly unguarded or else carefully and meticulously wrought, which
thus appears in what is usually deemed the most evangelical
of Pauline letters.[18]

Enough has been adduced to intimate the matrix from
which Christian worship emerged. The New Testament embodies evidence of what Walter Pater has called the church's
"wholly unparalleled genius for liturgy." [19] It contains compositions—psalms, canticles, and "spiritual songs"—some of
which continue in use even now.[20] The salutations and
blessings with which most of the Pauline and other letters
begin and end remind us that the correspondence was written to be read publicly in the service. There are explicit
declarations that the Lord's Prayer was to be used both as
a formal prayer and as a model of prayer.[21] Common worship abounded in prescribed affirmations such as, "Jesus is
Lord," "Amen," and "Maranatha." [22]

But even more striking is the realization that some New
Testament writings are, at least in part, products of that
genius to which Pater alluded. Archbishop Philip Carrington

has presented convincing evidence that the gospel according
to Saint Mark (and, for that matter, Saint Matthew) was
composed or arranged for reading Sunday by Sunday in
conformity with the Jewish agricultural year.[23] Miss Aileen
Guilding has similarly concluded that the gospel according
to Saint John "might fairly be described as a Christian commentary on the lections of the triennial cycle" of a Jewish
liturgical Kalendar.[24] Professor F. L. Cross has suggested
that I Peter, instead of being a letter, is an Easter homily de-
livered by an early Christian bishop on the occasion of a
baptism, or as he says, "a Paschal liturgy." [25]

That the book of Saint James has a real unity can be made
clear if it is understood as an episcopal address to a Jewish-
Christian liturgical assembly near the end of the first century. In it a visiting clergyman exhorts in turn the various
segments of the congregation as they are grouped in their
customary arrangement in early Christianity—first, the clergy: rulers (bishops) of the church, 1:2–27; deacons (door-
keepers and servers of tables), 2:1–26; and teachers (rabbis),
3:1–18; then the laity: widows and virgins, 4:1–10; penitents (slanderers, braggarts, carousers, impatient ones, oath-
takers), 4:11–5:12; and the faithful, 5:13–20.[26]

Not only were some writings of the New Testament in
part offspring of the liturgy, but the canon itself was a product. In the final analysis the canon that was ultimately accepted was made up of those books most often employed in
the service. Hence it was that many early Christian docu-
ments, just as instructive and valuable as those with canonical status, fell by the wayside and became, as it were, *apoc-
rypha*. Furthermore, it was probably liturgical use that
preserved certain apocryphal texts, for example, the *pericope adulterae* (John 7:53–8:11), the doxology of the Lord's
Prayer (Matthew 6:13), and possibly the longer ending of

Saint Mark (16:9–20). At a much later period it was liturgical usage that popularized certain versions of the Bible,
most notably Saint Jerome's Vulgate and Luther's translation. But the Book of Common Prayer maintains to this day
the Great Bible version of the Psalms. And it was incorporation of the Authorized (King James) Version into "Laud's
Liturgy" that promoted it in supplanting the Geneva Bible
in the latter's last stronghold, Scotland.

By mid-second century or thereabouts the Christian liturgy had reached a degree of stability in order if not in language, as implied by Saint Justin Martyr, but it was the same
as intimated earlier by Saint Ignatius of Antioch, the *Didache*, and Pliny's letter to Trajan, if not also by the Apocalypse. At this stage it was primarily the sacramental (baptismal and Eucharistic) rites of the church. But already it
was tending to expand. By the time of the peace of the
church the Divine Office was in embryonic existence, measured hymnody was being composed, and a Proper of saints,
in addition to that of time, was beginning, all of them logical
extensions of liturgy, indeed so inextricably linked with it as
to be identified with it. It is obvious therefore that the liturgy has always been enormously vital and creative,[27] so
much so that it would require special study to deal adequately with para-liturgical devotions that have emanated
from it. Suffice it here to mention only the Holy Rosary,
which in turn begot a liturgical festival in its honor.

By the sixth century there were also commentaries on
liturgy to explain it, justify it, and reinterpret it. These
served quite naturally to further its already powerful influence. In the ninth century there lived a man, Amalarius
of Metz,[28] who was almost oblivious to the world surrounding him, whose *magnum opus* was an elaborate treatise on
worship. In that work he discussed the familiar liturgy as

allegory and thereby invested it with a gossamer quality hitherto unknown. A man of originality and imagination, he sowed the seed destined to result about a century later in the liturgical drama.[29] It was once believed, then denied, that such drama grew from liturgy by way of the celebrated Saint Gall "Quem quaeritis"-trope.[30] Recently, however, the older view has been revived, reworked, and successfully reestablished by Professor O. B. Hardison, Jr.[31] So the liturgy gave rise to production of mysteries, miracles, and moralities, as it had already given birth to rhythmical, rhyming sequences, which would evoke secular parodies and imitations. Some of the plays were still being presented in the days of Shakespeare.

Sermons were another channel through which influence of the liturgy was explained. Originally loose, running comments on Gospel lections, they necessarily followed the recurring cycle of the ecclesiastical year. On saints' days they became tales about the lives of saints. By the high Middle Ages there were books of such stories for lazy preachers called "Sleepwells" (*dormi secure*). There was *The Golden Legend* of Jacobus da Varagine. There were collections of *exempla*, or illustrative material with pointed morals. There was the more entertaining volume known as *Gesta Romanorum*. These set a fashion for similar secular collections, becoming the immediate background of Boccaccio's *Decameron* and hence of Chaucer's *Canterbury Tales*.

It would be going astray here to mention ways in which the liturgy made its impact upon music,[32] folklore,[33] dogma,[34] architecture,[35] politics,[36] fraternal organizations,[37] and so forth. A few references are noted in the documentation that can lead the reader very far afield. My purpose is to spell out some specific details of relationship between liturgy and literature. Presented below therefore is a selection of some essays that I have prepared over a period of twenty years. It will be observed that I employ the term *liturgy* in a broad, not a narrow, signification. By it I often mean not only Mass, but also Divine Office, the Bible, preaching, the church year, and such expressions as the Rosary that have logically evolved.

The two initial topics—"The Worship of 'Most Primitive' Christianity" and "Early Christian Nighttime Worship"— illustrate, on the one hand, how features of the earliest Christian liturgy may be discerned through indications in the New Testament, and on the other, how it helped to shape the New Testament. They deal with a very distant period when liturgy was still relatively fluid and when the New Testament as such had not come into existence. The third and fourth topics—"A Fresh Exegesis of Mark 2:1–12" and "A Note on the Liturgy of the Apocalypse"—are concerned with a later interval when liturgy had reached some degree of stability. A significant element of the writers' background, it served as part of their frame of reference.

An emerging liturgical Kalendar is demonstrated by the fifth, sixth, and seventh topics—"Wisdom 18:14–15: An Early Christmas Text," "Christmas Echoes at Paschaltide," and "The Harrowing of Hell, Psalm 24, and Pliny the Younger: A Note"—which are based not only on Christian, but also on Jewish and pagan, sources. At the same time we may witness therein a steady growth of liturgy. The four papers assembled as the eighth topic—"Petronius and the Gospel before the Gospels?"—intimate how a cynical Roman author employed the *matière de Chrétienté* during years in which Christian writing was at a minimum, when information about the religion came chiefly from the spoken word. The remaining topics—"A Note on the Date of the Great Advent Antiphons," "*Beowulf* and the Liturgy,"

"Joseph of Arimathea and a Chalice," "Alleluia: A Word
and Its Effect," and "Shakespeare and the Holy Rosary"—
discuss works from subsequent centuries when the liturgy
not only had become fixed, but also had given rise to pro-
longations of itself in peripheral services and practices. It
and its corollaries had grown so familiar that writers alluded
both consciously and unconsciously to them.

1

The Worship

of "Most Primitive"

Christianity

From the score of years intervening between the crucifixion and the writing of the earlier Pauline letters there is extant no literary datum concerning the life, thought, and work of the church. Whatever may once have been recorded no longer exists. The very earliest extant source of such information is the Apostle's correspondence with the Galatians, Thessalonians, and Corinthians (that is, so-called II Corinthians). From statements, inferences, allusions, even silences in them, however, it is possible and proper to adduce testimony respecting organization, creed, code, and cult of the "most primitive" Christianity, if we remember always to employ the material cautiously. To deal even superficially with all of those topics would require many pages. Polity, doctrine, and ethics have often been treated extensively and perhaps adequately. Hence it is my purpose here to limit consideration to evidence of cultus, but it is inevitable that the other subjects be involved in the discussion (as indeed they are in actual life). It is my intention nonetheless

22   LITURGY AND LITERATURE

to permit reference to them only as they are related to liturgical expression.

By the time Saint Paul wrote, and no doubt much earlier, the church was already a highly complex institution. Parts of it, at least, had leaders called "pillars" (Galatians 2:9) and a clear division of labor (Galatians 2:7–9), as well as certain "minor orders" (in particular, one called "catechist"), members of which received compensation for their services (Galatians 6:6). There were "apostles" and their assistants (I Thessalonians 3:2), as well as "prophets" (I Thessalonians 5:20) and "readers" (I Thessalonians 5:27). A distinction between "clergy" and "laity" was thus made obvious, clergy having not only the duty of ministering but also the responsibility of governing and admonishing (I Thessalonians 5:12). The layfolk were urged to esteem and love their clergy and to keep in harmony and unity with them (I Thessalonians 5:12, Greek). Above all, the "brethren" were to abhor "undisciplined wanderers" who might lead them astray (II Thessalonians 3:6, if Pauline). So well organized indeed was the church that canonical censures could be imposed (II Thessalonians 3:14f.) and later (after due process) lifted (II Corinthians 2:6f.). But the most striking note of all is that within the two brief decades following the crucifixion the church was already being characterized as the "bride of Christ" (II Corinthians 11:2), as a "second Eve" (II Corinthians 11:3), and as God's "true Jewry" (Galatians 6:16; cf. 4:28, Philippians 3:3, Colossians 3:12).

Perhaps the last-mentioned description suggests a reason for such rapid development. The "earliest" church was predominantly Jewish, certainly in Palestine, but also in Asia Minor and in Europe, so much so that the great Apostle felt constrained to speak severely against continuance of some

Hebraic practices (Galatians 2). At the same time, however, he commended the Judean church as a model (I Thessalonians 2:14). Saint Paul himself is an illustration of the persistent impact of Judaism, notably in the employment of midrashic allegory (Galatians 4:22-30). In view therefore of the rather elaborate polity and remembering the importance of Jewish background, one will not be too surprised to find that worship was far from plain. As a matter of fact, most of the references given above might well have been cited as evidence of liturgical development.

One of the first things to note about the "most primitive" church was its use of an ecclesiastical Kalendar, presumably the old Jewish agricultural or liturgical calendar. The Galatian church, for example, was observing special days and months, special seasons and years (Galatians 4:10). Although Saint Paul's statement is ambiguous, it is probable that he intended to convey disapproval, but that interpretation is by no means assured. It appears that the Apostle himself may have adhered to many of the liturgical aspects of Judaism, such as Pasch (I Corinthians 5:7), Omer (I Corinthians 15:20), Shabuoth (I Corinthians 16:8), and possibly Succoth (II Corinthians 4:6, 17f.). It is quite certain that, conceding the aptness of some calendrical observances—new moons, sabbaths, and others—as being shadows of things to come, the substance of which was the Lord Himself, he bade his converts to allow no one to judge them in that respect (Colossians 2:16f.). It is in his writings that there occurs the first allusion to Christ's birth, a cryptic passage that is placed within an unusually appropriate setting referring to the time and circumstances (Galatians 4:4). For that reason one might almost suppose it to imply some kind of Nativity observance.[1]

In addition to liturgical arrangement ("array") and eccle-

siastical Kalendar, Saint Paul also attests some of the ceremonial acts of worship. The "holy kiss," or kiss of peace,
which was an expressive demonstration of the fellowship of
believers, was important enough to be four times mentioned
by him (I Thessalonians 5:26; II Corinthians 13:12; I Corinthians 16:20; Romans 16:16). This feature has persisted over
the centuries since then and continues today in an attenuated
form. It is possible that he intimates the use of incense a half-
century before it is referred to in the Apocalypse (II Corinthians 2:14–16; cf. Revelation 5:8). Triumphal display is
suggested (II Corinthians 2:14), as well as "splendor" (note
repetition of the word in I Corinthians 3:7–11) and the
sense of mystery (II Corinthians 4:3f.), all of which tended
to induce ecstatic conditions (II Corinthians 3:18; 4:6, 17f.;
cf. Galatians 6:14) and possibly even the Stigmata long
before Saint Francis of Assisi (Galatians 6:17;[2] cf. II Corinthians 4:10). But speculation staggers at the vista opened by
the Apostle's enigmatic remark that before the very eyes
(not ears) of the Galatians, Christ had been "depicted" or
"portrayed" (not proclaimed) as the Crucified One (Galatians 3:1).[3] Does he mean that "most primitive" churchmen
actually had representations of the crucifixion or that in
some manner the death of Christ was dramatized in their
presence? Or, just as strikingly, does he thus allude to the
Eucharistic or other church service? The words of this passage are strangely emphatic and surely do not refer merely
to the spoken word, however colorful and evocative it might
have been. In any case it begs the question to dismiss the
Pauline language as simply rhetorical or metaphorical.

Looking more closely at elements that comprise liturgy
in the narrower sense, one finds the earliest testimony to use
of the Lord's Prayer in worship in a passage that seems to
describe all prayer as "saying aloud, 'Abba,' that is, the

[Our] Father" (Galatians 4:6; cf. Romans 8:15).[4] There is also, as noted above, public reading of the Apostle's letters in the assembly (I Thessalonians 5:27), as well as some form of mutual prayer and of solemn blessing (I Thessalonians 1:1; 5:25, 28; Galatians 1:3–5; 6:18; II Thessalonians 1:2; 3:18; II Corinthians 1:3, and especially 13:14). A single verse—"For however many [or, however great] God's promises are, in Him [Christ] is their affirmation; wherefore also 'through Him' the Amen [is spoken] by us to God in respect of glory" (II Corinthians 1:20)—reveals, first, the solemn congregational utterance of Amen in the service; second, the formula "through Jesus Christ" as a fixed ending of prayer; and third, the quite Jewish characterization of true prayer as chiefly a glorifying or "blessing" of God. The remarkable verses immediately following—"The One who is strengthening us with you unto Christ and who has anointed us is God, who is also the One who has marked [sealed] us and has given the 'pledge' of the Spirit in our hearts" (II Corinthians 1:21f.)—seem to allude to the seal [*sphragis*] of Baptism, the chrism of Confirmation, and the grace of the Eucharist. The intimations of Baptism-Confirmation are fairly obvious; allusion to the Eucharist appears to be established by a further reference in the same letter where the Apostle assures his readers that to prepare them for immortality God gave them a spiritual "guarantee" (II Corinthians 5:5). Not long afterwards perhaps, Saint Paul varied the designation from "guarantee" to "first fruits" of the Spirit that a believer has while awaiting redemption of the body (Romans 8:23). Still later by several decades an enthusiastic Paulinist apparently understood these passages in a Eucharistic sense when he characterized the "pledge" of the Holy Spirit as a "token" of an inheritance not yet received in its fullness (Ephesians 1:13f.). In any event, the last step of this progressive interpretation was reached by Saint Ignatius of Antioch, who within a few years of the publication of the *corpus Paulinum* penned his well-known description of the Eucharist as "a drug of immortality, an antidote against dying." [5]

What has been presented thus far is derived from those letters of Saint Paul which are reputed to be the earliest. It is evident that liturgical usage in the earliest Christianity was not plain and unadorned, but quite rich. A glance at those letters which are deemed to be later will only ratify that conclusion. Some of these passages have already been cited, but a few additional ones may be permitted.

At the outset attention should be directed to an indication that a particular day of the week, the first or Sunday, was a special day of observance in the church (I Corinthians 16:2). What its precise significance was is ambiguous. The suggestions respecting organization are somewhat clearer. A distinction between major and minor "orders" is confirmed, and in addition to apostles and prophets the order of "doctor" (rabbi?) and other offices are noted (I Corinthians 12:28–30; Romans 12:4–8). The clergy are also identified as "bishops" and "deacons" (Philippians 1:1), and in one instance as sacrificial, sacerdotal ministrants (Romans 15: 16). Deference to the clergy is enjoined (I Corinthians 16:16). This ordering of the church into various ranks was necessary to maintain peace, unity, and stability in the Christian *ecclesia*. Partisan spirit was rife and it had to be quelled (I Corinthians 1:12; Philippians 1:15–18). Regulation was one method. Another was discipline, including the solemn procedure of excommunication and anathema (I Corinthians 5:4f., 13; 16:22).

In respect of ceremonial the language of mystery, awe, and drama was heightened (e.g., I Corinthians 2:8; Colossians 1:26; 2:16). Angels were said to be present at the worship of the liturgical assembly (I Corinthians 11:10), and unworthy participation in the Eucharist was said to have resulted in illness, debility, and even death (I Corinthians 11:30). The service bore some resemblance to a great sacrificial occasion either among the Jews or among the Levantine pagans (Romans 15:15; I Corinthians 10:21). Baptism was a miraculous occurrence like the crossing of the Red Sea and the Eucharist was a supernatural food like that supplied to the Israelites in the wilderness (I Corinthians 10:1–4). So tremendous indeed was the effect of Baptism that it was administered and received vicariously on behalf of persons long dead (I Corinthians 15:29). In fact, Baptism was a mysterious participation in Christ's atoning death and resurrection (Romans 6:3–11).

If Saint Paul was representative, the "most primitive" church was profoundly concerned about the *minutiae* of its liturgy, about its *schema* and *taxis*, its appropriate rationale and orderly array (I Corinthians 14:40). At one point the Apostle suggests a sequence of elements in the nonsacramental part of the service: proclamation of the Word (reading and preaching), affirmation of belief, and prayer (Romans 10:14f.). Something like a "creed" or catechetical exposition of the faith is presented (I Corinthians 15:3–8) and a ceremonial expression of affirmation (bowing) is recorded (Philippians 2:10f.).[6] Prayer is described as primarily *eulogia* and *eucharistia*, "blessing" and "thanksgiving," to which the congregation replies with the allusive Amen (I Corinthians 14:16). A traditional prayer in Aramaic is mentioned and was probably used in that language (I Corinthians 16:22; Philippians 4:6; cf. *Didache*, x, 6). A feature not mentioned earlier was the employment of music, that is, Psalmody, hymnody, and other compositions, at intervals of the service (Colossians 3:16). The Eucharistic portion of the liturgy is given in some detail with reference to the elements (the cup of wine and loaf of bread), to the words of distribution, and to the fraction and communication (I Corinthians 10:16f.; 11:23–26).

A final matter, also not mentioned in the earlier letters, is the fact that the liturgical assembly met in private homes (Romans 16:5; Colossians 4:15; Philemon 2). This practice, of course, suggests that the "most primitive" Christian service was very intimate, that only a small number (perhaps less than forty or fifty) participated in it at a given time, that each person had a distinct part to perform, and that the sense of participation was very impressive.

Even so brief a summary should serve to dispose of loose talk so often heard that early Christian worship was informal and colorless. The material here presented may be systematized in a series of propositions:

(1) The "most primitive" church (or liturgical assembly), characterized as "bride of Christ," "second Eve," God's "true Israel," an immediate, lawful, and lineal offspring of Judaism, was divided into two "orders," clergy and laity. The clergy was composed of "pillars," apostles and their assistants, prophets, bishops, deacons, "priests," catechists, doctors, and presumably others. The laity was simply designated as the "brethren."

(2) The "most primitive" church was empowered to impose both censure and absolution therefrom.

(3) The "most primitive" church had an ecclesiastical Kalendar consisting of special days (sabbaths), months (new moons), seasons, and years, specifically Pasch, Omer, Shabuoth, Succoth, Christmas (?), Sunday (and consequently Easter?).

(4) In its worship the "most primitive" church employed

splendor, mystery, portrayal (pictures? drama?), awe, pageantry.

(5) In its worship (Baptism-Confirmation, Eucharist) the "most primitive" church made use of reading, affirmation, mutual prayer and blessing, a formulaic ending for its prayers, the Lord's Prayer, the congregational Amen, and singing.

2

Early Christian
Nighttime Worship

In Saint Paul's earliest literary effort as in his latest, there occurs a figure of speech, curiously emphatic, employing imagery of night and day, of darkness and light.[1] In the former the Apostle states that, although night is ordinarily a time for sleep or revelry, Christians, as children of daylight, must remain awake and sober during the night and must also be suitably clothed as for warfare with the forces of darkness. In the latter passage the thought is virtually identical: let us spend our nights not as pagans do; let us rather abandon the ways of darkness and don armor befitting the dawn. So impressive indeed are his words that they suggest something other than a merely literary device. In fact they imply that the major Christian service of his time was celebrated during the hours of darkness or between dusk and dawn. Evidence for that practice in the first century, although somewhat inferential, is fairly strong.

The only service positively alluded to by the Apostle is the Eucharistic assembly,[2] which, because of reference to a supper of the Lord and because of the circumstance of its institution on the night in which He was betrayed, very likely took place during the hours of darkness. The other three accounts of the Eucharist,[3] although later than the Pauline record, are in agreement with it in preserving the tradition of institution at night. In the New Testament books written after Saint Paul indications of nighttime services appear to be even weightier. It is possible, for example, that the account relating to Nicodemus may reflect such an occasion.[4] If so, we have in it an intimation of the catechetical instruction that preceded baptism and was followed by a homily or sermon.

In the Matthean resurrection-story the statement that the guard was bribed to make ("his disciples came by night and stole him away"[5]) implies popular knowledge that Christian activity took place during the darkness. Two, possibly three, of the late accounts of resurrection-appearances seem to be narrated in Eucharistic terms. If so, we have further evidence of night assemblies for worship: the Lucan Emmaus-apparition that occurred in the evening twilight[6] ("first dark") and the Johannine Galilaean appearance that occurred in the twilight of early morning.[7] If the passage following the Emmaus account is to be reckoned here, its story belongs definitely to the night.[8]

When we turn to the book of Acts, we find a number of unambiguous instances that leave no doubt about the practice at the end of the first century. The church was praying ceaselessly for Saint Peter while he was in prison; when he was set free by angelic interference it was to a night assembly of the church that he went.[9] It was during the night that a religious service followed by the sacrament of baptism occurred in Philippi.[10] A quite noteworthy instance is the fairly detailed account of the service in Troas at which young

Eutychus fell asleep.[11] Several other passages may embody allusions to or reflections of the night services: the miraculous release of Saints Peter and John from prison during the night,[12] the two occasions of an angel's promise to Saint Paul in a vision that he would bear witness in Rome,[13] and the singularly intriguing incident of Saint Paul's *missa navalis* just before daybreak.[14]

If, as seems likely, I Peter is the "earliest documentation of a Christian service," a 'sacramentary' for the liturgy of baptism during the Easter Vigil,[15] we have therein further confirmation of important Christian observances during the nighttime. Again, if the Apocalypse reflects the Eucharistic rite of the primitive church,[16] it affords still further testimony. Indeed both I Peter and the Apocalypse exhibit very close affinities with the meager indications in the famous letter of Pliny the Younger.[17] These three works appear to supplement each other in describing the same kind of liturgical worship. And, if so, the evidence from Pliny is decisive that the major Christian services occurred between sundown and sunrise.

Apart from Pliny the witnesses thus far adduced are inevitably New Testament sources; Pliny, of course, provides a precious bit of pagan awareness of Christian practice. If we may credit the writings of Tertullian and Minucius Felix, it was common knowledge among pagans by the second half of the second century that the chief Christian services were celebrated during the night. The former speaks apparently from his own experience of rumors that were passing from person to person;[18] the latter cites inflammatory speeches of the prominent pagan orator, M. Cornelius Fronto.[19] Marcus Aurelius may allude to the secrecy of Christian assemblies, but he does not specifically mention the time.[20] In any case, the nature of the reports indicates that darkness of night was virtually an integral part of Christian worship. It was that fact indeed which presumably gave the reports sufficient color for popular credence. The Eucharist during the hours between dusk and dawn, a meeting by candlelight or lamplight, the kiss of peace, perhaps a baptism with its disrobing and reclothing, the use of familial language—all might easily give rise to wildly imagined "Thyestean banquets and Oedipodean orgies." On the other hand, it is difficult to conceive of anything else in Christian practice that would have led to such fantastic charges.

For almost two centuries, therefore, the words of Saint Paul mentioned at the beginning of this paper had quite realistic connotations as they were read, reread, and expounded in the primitive Christian assemblies. We can understand also the realism of the strange word *epiousion* used in the petition for bread in the Lord's Prayer, that is, bread for the day which is at hand.[21] But we may well ask the reasons underlying Christian predilection for nighttime services. After all, the tradition did not persist on a significant scale after the peace of the church. And, moreover, the vast majority of regular non-Christian services, Jewish or pagan, with which the early Christians might have been acquainted were, generally speaking, daytime performances.[22] Consequently there must have been ample cause to impel the primitive church to adopt the dark hours for its customary services of worship.

The first motives were no doubt the so-called practical ones. The earliest Christians were a humble group, not many of whom "were wise according to worldly standards, not many were powerful, not many were of noble birth." [23] Their days were spent in hard labor and only the nights were available for their special religious services. In their world work belonged specifically to the daytime, but at nightfall, "when no one can work," [24] they were relatively free. Moreover, as time passed and the new movement came to be looked upon with increasing disfavor, it was expedient because of fear to meet at night to avoid hostile prying eyes.[25]

Once the fact of meeting at night was an established usage, there would develop certain "reasons" to explain the practice. These were both allegorical and theological. Saint Paul's remark, "You . . . know well that the day of the Lord will come like a thief in the night," [26] seems to belong to the sphere of allegory. It is, of course, either a contradiction or a paradox unless it is taken within the imaginative context of allegory, but within that framework it is a very striking statement. The theological motivation is quite similar. There seems to have been a widespread belief that the Parousia of the Lord would occur at night.[27] Hence the need for vigil through the hours between sunset and sunrise. "Watch therefore lest He come suddenly and find you asleep; for you do not know when the Master of the house is coming, at twilight, or midnight, or cock-crow, or dawn." [28] This belief is reflected in the parable of the wise and foolish virgins.[29] It may also give poignancy to the Apocalyptic promise that after the Parousia "night shall be no more" [30] and to the pseudo-Petrine exhortation to give heed to prophecy "until the day dawns and the morning star rises in your hearts." [31]

After the "practical" and theoretical reasons, a third is imitation. So much that is recorded of Christ's life took place during the night that the early Christians must have deemed their own practice to have been part of a general *imitatio Christi.* Jesus frequently spent nights in prayer.[32] Some of His miraculous apparitions were at night.[33] He was indeed said to have been born at night,[34] and it was during the night that He was spirited away from Bethlehem to Egypt.[35] Liturgically a striking passage from the Old Testament was quite early applied to the circumstances of Christ's birth: "While all things were in quiet silence, and that night was in the midst of her swift course, Thine almighty Word leaped down from heaven out of Thy royal throne. . . ."[36]

This passage, or rather its context, brings to mind the Jewish feast of Passover and suggests that Christians may also have been consciously imitating certain infrequent but infinitely important Judaic observances that had their climaxes at night rather than in daytime.[37] The fact that the Passover was primarily an evening or night ceremony and the fact that the chief Christian ceremony was derived from it were undoubtedly compelling motives for the church to continue to have its greater liturgical worship after sunset and before sunrise.

Far more profound, however, must have been the influence of the feast commonly called Tabernacles. Christianity converted Passover into Easter, Shabuoth into Pentecost, and even Chanukkah into Christmas and Epiphany, but it failed to introduce anything like Tabernacles permanently into its sacred year, though that celebration was in some respects the most significant of all Jewish festivals. (But perhaps that was the very reason why Christians eliminated it from their calendar.) The pinnacle of the occasion was an all-night illumination of the women's court of the Temple, an accompanying torch-dance, and a procession of priests just before dawn.[38] Christ had apparently applied the observance to Himself.[39] Though the feast itself had no analogue in Christianity, its impact is discernible in many parts of the New Testament.[40] The early church therefore certainly had adequate authority to imitate it at least in part.

With cessation of persecution and with imperial recognition of the church, Christianity had no urgent need for night services. There was no longer cause for fear and secrecy, nor, with acceptance of Sunday as a legal day of rest, any necessity for workers to wait for nightfall to attend service. Even so the weight of tradition was by then too strong to allow complete abandonment of worship at night. It lingered most notably in the nocturnal office of monasticism today called Matins, most elaborate of the canonical Hours. But somewhat more striking was the persistence of occasions when Mass was said at night, the vigil of Easter being perhaps the original such occasion, preserving many ancient customs of nighttime services.[41] When Christmas became part of the sacred year, it gradually superseded Easter in popularity and also developed its own midnight and early morning liturgy. On the model of Christmas, Summer Saint John's Day also had for a while its special nocturnal Mass.[42] (Both of these no doubt reflect some accommodation to pagan observance of the solstices.) There was at least one more or less local commemoration which also drew to itself similar solemnity, namely, the feast of Saint Justus at Lyons, aptly described by Sidonius Apollinaris.[43] But apart from these lingering practices, somewhat old-fashioned, daylight has long since replaced night as the customary time of Christian worship.

3

A Fresh Exegesis

of Mark 2:1–12

The most interesting, and it may well be the most fruitful, recent development in Biblical criticism is the discernment of liturgical motifs embedded in or underlying the books of the New Testament. A significant and refreshing result of this research is the renewed awareness that Christian preaching, sacramental ministrations, and worship, in all their ramifications, antedated the earliest writings of the New Testament by at least a score of years, the latest by as much as a century, and its ultimate canonization by perhaps a third of a millenium. We have rediscovered the truth that the Christian church preceded the New Testament, that the New Testament is therefore a documentary source of information about the life of the Apostolic church, and, above all, that the New Testament is itself a phase of the Holy Tradition.

The importance of this interpretation may be briefly illustrated by the following tentative exegesis of a familiar passage. A careful examination of the language employed in the pericope, Mark 2:1–12, seems to reveal a sacramental or liturgical motivation.

Verse 2. "many were gathered together." The word *sunechthesan* (from *sunago*) suggests a "synagogal" assembly for worship and instruction. "And he was preaching the word." The translation "was preaching" does not do justice to *elalei*, which means "is speaking ecstatically." Nor is *ton logon* merely "the word." It is the "reasoned discourse" or even "sermon."

Verse 3. "bringing to him." Here are the components of *prospherentes*, "making an oblation" or "offering (a sacrifice)." "They" are unidentified.

Verse 4. "could not get near . . . because of the crowd." Possibly, "being unable to make the oblation (or, offer a sacrifice) . . . because of the crowd." Whoever "they" are, "they" finally "unroof the roof" (note the play on words) *where Christ is*—that is, as though entering a Holy of Holies or appearing before the Real Presence of God—and let down the pallet on which the paralytic lay (the action recalls Acts 10:10–16). "They" are vaguely identified as friends of the paralytic, the bearers of his pallet.

Verse 5. "saw their faith." Undoubtedly "their" refers especially to the (four) friends, but may include the paralytic. It is important to observe that "their faith" was exhibited or recognized only when they were apart from the crowd and in the Veritable Presence of the Lord; and similarly it was only thus that Christ addressed the paralytic as "son." A clear distinction is therefore made between the assembled multitude with which the pericope began and the small inner group at the heart of the account. "your sins are forgiven." A bold, immediate, positive reality. But note that the statement refers to a purely spiritual, invisible, intangible effect that took place away from the crowd, after a solemn discourse, in the Very Presence, where faith was obvious, and where the true brotherhood of believers had been confirmed by the Divine adoption.

Verses 6-9. *Inter alia*, the scribes questioned the reality of the spiritual occurrence. Their obtuseness required an external sign.

Verse 10. "that you may know." An acknowledgement of the value of an external testimony. Here is, in all but the very words, the old description of a sacrament as "an outward and visible sign of an inward and spiritual grace given unto us."

Verses 11, 12. "I say to you. . . . And he rose." The visible token, an instantaneous, palpable change, in obedience to a creative (or recreative) *fiat* of the Lord. "amazed." That is "ecstatic" or "(divinely) frenzied." A reaction comparable to an outpouring of the Holy Spirit. "glorified God." Apparently meaning, perceived and expressed the glory of God.

With the passage before us, let us proceed further. The decisive words are those in verse 4, *dia ton ochlon*, "because of the crowd." The bearers of the paralytic came to accomplish a certain purpose, but the presence of the throng prevented fulfillment; away from the multitude, however, in the presence of Christ, the purpose was achieved. These words therefore constitute a division in the story: something happened after them which could not have happened before them. We may inquire what that "something" was. As we have seen above, it was an "oblation" or "offering" of some kind. But the words, *dia ton ochlon*, mark another division. Before them, the scene was that of a throng listening to an impressive discourse. Afterward, there was an occurrence with both inward and outward effects, evoking from the observers an expression of wonderment and praise (or adoration).

The most primitive form of the liturgy was twofold: the first part consisting of Scriptural lections and homilies, being open to all those who were sufficiently interested to be present; the second part, consisting of the Eucharist, being open only to attested believers. The two parts had appropriate names: the first was called "Mass of the catechumens" (*Missa catechumenorum*) or "that which precedes the oblation" (Pro-Anaphora); the second was designated "Mass of the faithful" (*Missa fidelium*) or the "oblation" (Anaphora). Recently they have been more simply denominated the "Liturgy of the Word" and the "Liturgy of the Upper Room." Anciently at the end of the readings and sermon occurred the "expulsion of the catechumens," only baptized Christians in good standing remaining for Communion. The first portion, open to the public, had some of the characteristics of a missionary or evangelistic meeting. But the second, the sacramental, was for the brotherhood of believers only. The account of the Eucharist in Justin Martyr's *Apology* does not specifically mention the removal of the unbaptized, although the twofold division is evident, but the earliest liturgical forms and perhaps the Book of Revelation (see the following essay) do so quite clearly. The oblation, according to Saint Justin, belongs properly to the second part: he says that the bread and wine-mixed-with-water are "offered" (*prospheretai*) at the beginning of the *Missa fidelium*.

Returning now to our Gospel-pericope, we observe that the allusions in verses 2 and 3—the "synagogal" assembly of a multitude listening to the ecstatic proclamation of the Word—correspond neatly to the Pro-Anaphora. Moreover, the succession of ideas in verses 4–12 (the withdrawal into a "holy of holies," the oblation, the community of faith, the recognition of believers' sonship to God, the spiritual experience of forgiveness, the external miracle of vitality, the outburst of astonished praise) is remarkably similar to the progression of the *Missa fidelium*. It seems entirely reasonable therefore to suppose that the stylistic composition of this passage was framed in accordance with the basic order of the primitive Christian Eucharist.

How apt the literary structure is becomes apparent upon closer consideration of the spiritual teaching that it embodies. First, there is the urgency of inquirers who seek until their search is rewarded—a thought that is voiced many times and in many ways in the New Testament. Second, there are the doubts and questionings, the desire for palpable signs, the unbelief that is so close to faith—all these ideas are also often recorded in the New Testament. Third, there is the merciful compassion of the Savior who eagerly reaches out to fulfill the faint beginnings of movement toward God. Fourth, there is the demonstration of the Deity of Christ, who exercised the Divine prerogative when He knew what was in the hearts of men, performed a miracle of healing, and forgave sins. Here is the fourfold "shape of the liturgy," its inner movement of oblation, consecration, fraction, and communion: the offering of "our selves, our souls and bodies, to be a reasonable, holy, and living sacrifice"; the hallowing that, beyond all faith and doubt, "eucharistizes" the offering so that it is no longer something common; the giving of the Divine Body in mercy "for us men and for our salvation"; and the participation of believers in the supernatural life of God. Thus the basic teaching of this pericope confirms the literary principle as being sacramental and liturgical.

4

A Note

on the Liturgy

of the Apocalypse

There was a strange vitality in the early church that caused it to grow from a mere handful of timid converts into an empire; a magical fascination that made despairing mortals, lost in a vast military dictatorship, turn to it, cling to it, and be transformed by it into triumphant victors over the crushing burden of life; a magnetic grip that enabled most of its members to prefer torture and death to apostasy. Shortly after the turn of the first century after Christ, the pagan governor of Bithynia in Asia Minor, Pliny the Younger, wrote to the emperor in Rome a letter bearing eloquent, if exaggerated, testimony to this fact. "Many people." he says,

> of all ages, of every rank of society, and of both sexes are being endangered by this manifestation. . . . For this contagious superstition has permeated not only the cities but also the villages and even the countryside. It appears that suitable measures must be taken to stop and correct it. Surely our temples, now desolate, must be reopened; the sacred solemnities, long neglected, must be revived; and the sacri-

ficial offerings, both grain and animal, of which there has
been only the most occasional purchaser for a number of
years, must be brought to market. I think,

he hopes vainly, "it might be fairly easy for the majority of
the people to come to their senses, if an opportunity is presented for them to recant." [1]

What was the almost incredible attraction exerted by the
Christian church that could evoke such a statement from a
cultured and intelligent provincial official? Why did a Roman citizen

leave the marble temples, the accumulated statues and paint-
ings of all the centuries, the stately ceremonial, the white-
robed priest and the incense, the grave honourable well-
born men and women, thronging the sanctuary? Why leave
these people, whose mere conformity with the ancient
ritual, however superficial or careless, grouped them around
the daily sacrifices into a picture more impressive than any
on the walls of the temple itself? For . . . Pagan worship,
under that Southern sun, must have been . . . picturesque. [2]

Why indeed, unless for something more impelling? Not the
least interesting aspect of the Roman governor's letter to his
ruler is the implied comparison of two ways of worship, that
of the old gods and that of the Christian God.

It is coming to be generally recognized that the author of
the Apocalypse presents his visions, at least in part, against
the background or within the framework of the church
liturgy of the latter years of the first Christian century. [3]
Startling witness to the powerful grip, the persuasive attraction, the appealing vitality that this liturgy had for the minds
and hearts of the early Christians is thus borne by the Revelator whose every thought, conscious or not, seems to be
dominated by it. In order to visualize the ritual and ceremonial that held him in thralldom it will be well to take as a
point of reference the earliest clear-cut description of Chris-

tian worship that has come down to us: it occurs in the
(First) *Apology* of Saint Justin Martyr, about the middle of
the second century, or only a brief fifty years after the close
of the New Testament canon.[4]

Justin gives two accounts of the service: one, a Eucharist after a baptism; the other, the normal service of every
Sunday.[5] The customary sequence of weekly worship, with
details supplied from the postbaptismal rite, begins with the
reading of Scripture by one or more Lectors, prolonged as
time and circumstance permit. The lessons are from the
Memoirs of the Apostles, also called Gospels, or the writings
of the Prophets. Afterward, the "president of the brethren" [6] delivers a homily, admonishing and exhorting the
people to imitation of the excellent things they have just
heard from the Readers. The homily is followed by prayers
in some way offered in common by the entire assembly
standing. These prayers, which seem to be primarily intercessions, are offered for the worshipers, for the newly baptized if any are present, and for all men, that they may be
accounted worthy as living righteously in keeping with the
commandments, and that all may be partakers of everlasting
salvation.

Following the intercessions, the kiss of peace is given (men
to men and women to women, of course) and there is
brought to the "president" bread and a cup of wine-mixed-
with-water. The "president" thereupon offers prayer and
thanksgiving "according to his ability," to which the congregation expresses assent by responding with the *Amen*.
After this prayer comes communication of the bread and
cup of wine-mixed-with-water distributed by the deacons,
and the service is abruptly concluded. The deacons, however, carry away some of the sacred elements to those who
were unable to attend the service.

Since Saint Justin was directing his *Apology* to Emperor Antoninus Pius, that is, to a non-Christian reader, his language is largely untechnical. For example, his use of the word *president* is an obvious metonymy for *bishop* and the *brethren* are presumably the bishop's fellow-presbyters. Moreover, Justin makes no mention of singing, yet in all likelihood Psalms and canticles were used in the Christian assemblies, as we learn from Roman Pliny and from the epistles of the New Testament.[7] Still further, in the Justinian account, we can observe a twofold division of the service: an instructional part composed of readings and exhortation; and the sacramental part consisting of prayers and the Communion. This harks back to the description of Pentecost in the book of Acts, where the new converts are said to have "continued steadfastly in the Apostles' doctrine and fellowship, and in breaking of bread, and in prayers." [8] At a later date these two divisions were called respectively the Liturgy of the Catechumens (*Missa catechumenorum*, Pro-Anaphora) and the Liturgy of the Faithful (*Missa fidelium*, Anaphora), all interested persons being admitted to the former, but only baptized true believers to the latter. Some scholars trace this dichotomy to two separate sources, the first being in part derived from Jewish worship, the other from a distinctly Christian element added by the Lord.

Let us now return about half a century to the publication of the mysterious book of Revelation, a product of Asia Minor, probably written by an exiled and persecuted member of the clergy of Ephesus, and see if we can discern through its bizarre language the service of worship that seems to be hovering in the background. Consideration should first be given to the arrangement of the scene where the liturgy of heaven takes place. A most elaborate description is presented in Revelation 4 and 5, and many further

details are added in other portions of the book which con-
stantly refer to this scene. Presumably in the eastern part of
the meeting place[9] there is a central throne on which sits the
Eternal One. On each side, forming a semicircle, are twelve
similar thrones, occupied by twenty-four presbyters. Close
by the central throne are four creatures like those of Ezekiel's vision and reminiscent of Isaiah's seraphim.[10] The
author apparently had in mind the first sight that met the
eye of a person entering a Christian religious assembly for
the Eucharistic service: the presiding bishop, flanked by his
fellow-presbyters, and attended or assisted by his servant-
deacons. The letters of Saint Ignatius of Antioch (*ca.* 110–
117), only a few short years later than the Apocalypse, refer a number of times to the bishop in the place of God,
presbyters in the place of the council of Apostles, and deacons in the bishop's immediate service.[11] Justin Martyr, as
already noted, although not as full and technical in his
language, mentions the bishop (presumably) as "president
of the brethren" (presbyters) and calls special attention to
the serving function of the deacons.[12] Clement of Rome,
almost exactly contemporary with the Apocalyptic writer,
uses Old Testament verbiage with the same implication
when he says in his (First) *Letter to the Corinthians:* "To
the high priest have been given his proper 'liturgies'; to the
priests have been given their proper place; and on the Le-
vites have been imposed their proper 'deaconings'." [13]

In front of the main throne and on the chord of the arc
formed by the other thrones are, so the Apocalyptist says,
three objects, seven lampstands with their lights, a laver of
water, and an altar.[14] The lamps at once recall the famous
letter of Pliny to Trajan that states that the Christians were
accustomed to meet before dawn;[15] hence the need for arti-
ficial lights. The laver suggests the close association of the

sacraments of baptism and Eucharist mentioned by Saint Ignatius,[16] Saint Justin,[17] and the *Didache* (*ca.* 100),[18] and also the vague allusion of Pliny to the Christian renunciation of certain crimes.[19] The altar, or table, is, of course, a practical necessity for the sacrament of Holy Communion,[20] but here it also faintly intimates an early Christian practice of meeting in cemeteries and using the tomb of a martyr as a place for celebration of the Eucharist.[21]

On the other (the western) side of the altar-table, facing bishop and presbyters, and completing the circle around the altar, laver, and lamps, stand serried ranks of worshipers in their proper array: the Revelator lists them as martyrs and confessors,[22] virgins,[23] and the others.[24] Of this decent or fitting orderliness, Clement remarks thus: "Brethren, let each of us, having a good conscience, 'make Eucharist' to God in his own peculiar rank, reverently observing the prescribed rule of his 'liturgy'." [25] It is moreover to this beautiful decorum that Saint Ignatius exhorts the Ephesians:

> It is fitting that you keep harmonious step with the will of your bishop, as indeed you do. For thus your very famous college of presbyters is attuned to the bishop as strings to a lute. . . . Join this choir, each of you, that being harmoniously in concord you, having received the [musical] key of God in unison, may sing with one voice to the Father. . . .[26]

The scene then, as portrayed by the Apocalyptist, is a remarkable parallel to the scene of Christian worship as suggested by Clement and Ignatius, his contemporaries, and as described by Justin a half-century later. The day on which this liturgy is celebrated is surely Sunday, clearly stated by the *Didache* and Ignatius, implied by Pliny, and confirmed by Justin Martyr.[27] We return next to the order or rationale of the service as indicated by the book of Revelation.

Public reading of the Old Testament, of the letters of

Saint Paul, and of other Scriptures, as well as of letters from other bishops and doctors of the church is well attested without additional evidence and is mentioned in the Apocalypse, although it is probably impossible to identify the particular volume that the Lion-Lamb reads.[28] The festive solemnity here attending the reading is also implied by Pliny's reference to the Christians singing to Christ as to a god and by Justin's statement that such reading was extended as long as time permitted.[29] It is also possible and indeed probable that the Apocalyptist intends to intimate that the reading was accompanied or followed by impromptu exposition or a homily.

Thus we have the sequence of Scripture (and other readings) and a homily interspersed with singing. Next follows prayer.[30] Once again this is the order given more fully and more clearly by Saint Justin.[31] Significantly enough this is still the order nearly three centuries later that we observe at such great length in the *Apostolic Constitutions* (*ca.* 380).[32] The fact that the section from chapter 8, verse 6, through chapter 20 of the Apocalypse portrays in successive visions an account of war in heaven and on earth between God and His followers and the Evil One and his myrmidons suggests the distinction between unbaptized hearers admitted to the public part of the service and the faithful who alone may participate in the Eucharist. We have, as it were, a lengthy version of the "dismissal of the catechumens" quite comparable to the account in the *Apostolic Constitutions* of the expulsion of the catechumens, the demon-possessed, those on the eve of baptism, and penitents. But, in fact, these chapters of the book of Revelation, except for frequently repeated references to the scene of worship as described above, are not especially explicable by recourse to liturgical practice.[33]

Yet the recurring allusions keep us reminded of the framework of worship.

It is only when we come to chapters 21–22:5 that we seem once more to be certainly dealing with a liturgical background. Here, however, the description is particularly cryptic, far more so than in the earlier chapters. We seem to have here a conflation of the two sacraments of the New Covenant, or rather the portrayal of one (the Eucharist) in terms of the other (baptism). The glassy laver in front of the bishop's (God's) throne seems to have become a life-giving fountain from which flows a river of water through the congregation of worshipers, who have been transfigured into a vast holy city, the new Jerusalem. And along the banks of the crystalline stream grow miraculous fruitbearing trees of life and healing. Yet this very scene is also referred to as a wedding banquet and the allusions point to eating and drinking, not to a washing.[34] In spite of the apparent confusion, the scene suggests the strange phrase by which Ignatius characterized the Eucharist, "a drug of deathlessness, an antidote against dying." [35]

There are several explanations of the cryptic quality of the Apocalyptic utterance. First, it should never be forgotten that the book is after all not a factual analysis, but a prophetic vision in which many weird things may and do happen. Second, theologically the two sacraments are a unity: the substance of both is the same, namely, the Lord Himself, and the meaning of both is the same, namely, eternal life through participation in His victory over death. Third, there is indeed a liturgical unity of these sacraments, that is, admission to the Eucharist presupposes holy baptism.[36] Moreover, the earliest description of the Eucharist, as given by Justin Martyr, is of one that followed immediately after a baptism. Fourth (and perhaps the best explanation of all), even in the last decade of the first century there was probably good reason for caution in picturing the Christian Eucharist in a document that was an inflammatory broadside against the imperial Roman government. If, about A.D. 113, the sophisticated patrician governor of Bithynia (whose knowledge about the subject was derived from renegades, one of whom had apostatized as many as twenty years before) thought it proper to inform his emperor that the ritual meal of which the Christians partook was merely "ordinary and innocent" food, the implication is clear that already gossip was afloat about such macabre enormities as "Thyestean meals and Oedipodean intercourse" practiced in the sinister secrecy of Christian gatherings.[37] Even fifty years afterward Saint Justin felt impelled to explain to Antoninus Pius that there was no relationship between the Christian Eucharist and the harmless, but diabolically inspired, Mithraic initiatory banquet.[38] It is therefore quite likely that by the end of the first Christian century it was becoming advisable not to discuss the Eucharist except in guarded and veiled language. At any rate the passages by Justin Martyr are the only plain liturgical description until after the peace of the church. Even the brief report by Pliny is either garbled by his informants or contemptuously misunderstood by him.

If, however, we may assume that we do have here at least the suggestion of the Eucharist, it follows that in the Apocalypse we have essentially the same sequence or rationale of the Christian liturgy that is simply more adequately portrayed by Saint Justin Martyr: Scripture, homily, prayer, Eucharist. We also have details unmentioned by him, that is, the use of song between the readings of Scripture, suggested by Pliny, and perhaps also the dismissal of the unbaptized and the unfaithful, as noted in later patristic works. Surely it is unnecessary to point out that the most important element in worship is what is done and how it is done, that is, the rationale, the orderly sequence, rather than the ritual (the precise words used), ceremonial (the smaller actions), or the external "trappings" (vestments, colors, lights, incense, and the like). The words, ceremonies, and paraments may vary greatly within limits, particularly from culture to culture and from language to language, but the systematic flow of the several components of the liturgy, ever moving toward a definite goal, may not be altered without violating the universal tradition of the church.

The scheme discernible in the Apocalypse and in Saint Justin provides a basic outline that, with natural growth, has remained the underlying rationale of Eucharistic worship ever since. The prolonged reading of Scripture developed into the threefold pericopes of Prophecy, Epistle, and Gospel (shortened in time to Epistle and Gospel, except on certain occasions). The natural, informal homily became the reasoned discourse or sermon. The bringing forward of the bread and cup of wine-and-water was soon accompanied by an Offertory Psalm and Offertory prayers, and followed by "secret" prayers over that portion of the elements "separated" for use in the service.[39] The prayer and thanksgiving of consecration developed into *Sursum corda*, Preface, *Sanctus, Benedictus qui venit*, and Canon, into which the intercessions were also incorporated. The communication was soon accompanied by a Communion Psalm and followed by post-communion prayers. Two important additions were made that derived inevitably and naturally from practical necessity. The first was the entrance of the ministrants into the place of worship while an Introit Psalm was sung. The second was the formal dismissal of the people with a blessing at the end of the service and departure of the clergy. So the skeleton was clothed with the disproportionate length of an Oriental Eucharist lasting three hours in its fullness, or with the brief, almost curt, completeness of the Western rites that need not consume more than half an hour. But the point to be stressed is that however rich and full the liturgy became, or whatever pruning it received, it still has basically the same rationale we have discovered in Justin and in the Apocalypse.

The logical growth produced not a different liturgy, but the same more fully and adequately expressed. Neither was it a liturgy "imposed" by an authority other than Christian practice. It came into being in much the same manner as the canon of the New Testament. Both were officially confirmed only after having been sanctioned by usage, more or less in accordance with the commonsense *dictum* of Saint Vincent of Lérins, "quod semper, quod ubique, quod ab omnibus." If the guidance of the Holy Spirit means anything, surely it may be discerned as well in the formation of the traditional Christian liturgy as in the establishment of the New Testament canon.

For the sake of making the basic outline of the liturgy in the Apocalypse stand out in its clarity, this paper has deliberately bypassed the wealth of color, odors, hieratic language, and dramatic ceremonial provided by the Apocalyptic writer in his vision of worship. Such matters may be treated at a later time, but, however secondary or even tertiary, they should certainly not be overlooked.[40] For it was perhaps these very details that gave warmth to the service, that prove it was not something drab and bare, and that served as the germ of future ornamentation of the Christian liturgy.

5

Wisdom 18:14–15:

An Early Christmas Text

In the current *Missale Romanum* the Introit of Mass for Sunday within the Octave of Christmas, if it falls on December 29, 30, or 31, is a passage (slightly emended) from Wisdom 18:14–15, as follows:

> Dum medium silentium tenerent omnia, et nox in suo cursu medium iter haberet, omnipotens sermo tuus, Domine, de caelis a regalibus sedibus venit.[1]

It is rendered into English thus: "While all things were in quiet silence, and night was in the midst of her swift course, Thine almighty Word, O Lord, leaped down from heaven out of Thy royal throne." [2] The same sentence is also the Introit of Mass for the second Sunday after Christmas, which by tradition is perpetually reposed on the Vigil of Epiphany.[3] As indicated in the notes to the Latin quotation above, it is moreover employed in the Benedictine *Breviarium Monasticum* as an antiphon, first, on *Magnificat* at first Vespers of the Sunday within Christmas Octave (if it falls on December 29, 30, or 31), then on *Benedictus* at Lauds of

the Vigil of Epiphany.[4] In the twelfth and thirteenth centuries it was still further used as the antiphon on *Benedictus*
at Lauds of the Sunday after Christmas.[5]

At first glance the language of the Wisdom passage appears to be peculiarly apt for Christmastide: the "quiet silence" of the holy night "in the midst of her swift course"
and the mighty leap of the "almighty Word" from the
"royal throne" of heaven certainly constitute a beautiful,
mystical suggestion of the Incarnation. That is, until one
turns to read the context of the verse in the book of Wisdom. It is shocking to discover that the particular night "in
the midst of her swift course" was the night in which the
children of Israel left the land of Egypt, that the "quiet silence" was soon rent by the despairing wails of Egyptian
parents lamenting their firstborn,[6] and that the "almighty
Word" was not the Babe of Bethlehem but the Destroying
Angel wreaking havoc among the minions of Pharaoh.[7]

One cannot but marvel at the artistic genius of the person
who first wrenched this passage from its context and with
violent change of meaning applied it to the liturgy of
Christmas. Unfortunately identification of the brilliant compiler eludes us. So do the time and locality of the association.
We may nevertheless be sure that when the association was
made the liturgy was already tending to seasonal observances, hence toward formation of the so-called Proper of
Time, and moreover that the festival of Nativity was already being celebrated in some manner, however rudimentary. It is customary to date both of those developments
during and after the fourth century.[8] It is true that unambiguous attestation of both developments comes after the
peace of the church. Yet interest in Christ's birth and its
attendant circumstances began much earlier.

By the end of the first century there were in existence the

fairly elaborate accounts in the canonical gospels of Saints
Matthew and Luke.[9] If Archbishop Carrington's thesis is
true, they are evidence that a distinctively Christian yearly
cycle of services had already superseded the Jewish calendar.[10] Even more impressive, however, is the interest illustrated by the mystic retelling of the Nativity story in Revelation 12.[11] That passage is of special importance: while the
accounts in Matthew and Luke purport, at least, to be historical narratives, the Apocalyptic version indicates that the
Nativity was already invested with theological and liturgical interpretation.[12] To this may be added several passages
from later books of the New Testament: two allusions in
Titus to the appearance of "the goodness and lovingkind-
ness of God our Savior";[13] a similar reference in Hebrews
within the context of worship;[14] and, above all, a significant
mention of the Incarnation in a fragmentary early Christian
hymn incorporated in I Timothy.[15] Testimony for a profound devotion centering about the Nativity is firmly established by publication of "infancy gospels," the earliest
and best of which, the *Protevangelium of James*, was current in the second century.[16] The evidence seems, therefore,
to be sufficiently strong to suggest that as early as the beginning of the second century Christmas was in some manner
recognized and celebrated by the church and, consequently,
that the Christian liturgy already possessed the elements of
the Proper of Time.

   If our reasoning thus far is substantial, we may be able to
demonstrate that Wisdom 18:14–15 had been torn from its
context and appropriated for liturgical use during Christmastide by the end of the first century. It seems possible,
even probable, that this passage *with its Nativity application*
lurks in the background of a very early second century
work, namely, the epistle of Bishop Ignatius of Antioch to

the Ephesians, nineteenth chapter.[17] There are in the Ignatian passage a number of verbal echoes of the eighteenth chapter of Wisdom. Most noteworthy examples are the "still silence" *(hesuchou siges)* of Wisdom and "in the stillness of God" *(hesuchiai theou)* of Ignatius;[18] "perplexed them" *(exetaraxan)* and "perplexity" *(tarache)*;[19] "not knowing" *(agnoountes)* and "ignorance" *(agnoia)*;[20] perhaps "providest . . . for hospitality" *(xeneteias paresches)* and "provided a novelty" *(xenismon pareichen)*;[21] and several less important words.[22]

More significant than verbal parallels is similarity in sequence of ideas. First, Wisdom 18:1–19 mentions four vital truths that were hidden from the Egyptians: a very great light shining upon Israel,[23] rescue of the infant Moses,[24] the sacrifices and covenant of Israel,[25] and the fact that Israelites were sons of God.[26] Similarly Ignatius states that certain mysteries were kept secret from the prince of this age, in this case three: Mary's virginal conception, her Fruit (or, her childbearing), and the Lord's death.[27] Secondly, in Wisdom the manifestation of these hidden things occurs in the quiet silence,[28] at midnight,[29] through a destroying instrument of God's vengeance,[30] and by evocation of terrified perplexity.[31] In like manner, Ignatius, too, describes the revelation of his hidden things as taking place in the stillness of God by the appearance of a preternatural star, unutterably bright, whose novelty caused astonishment.[32] Thirdly, the results of the manifestation were, according to Wisdom, the wailing dirge of the bereft Egyptians,[33] end of deluding enchantments,[34] wholesale death,[35] and horrible dreams.[36] Results of the manifestation, according to Ignatuis, were the removal of magic, wickedness, ignorance, and the "old kingdom," and ultimately the destruction of death itself.[37] The concatenation of ideas is virtually the same in both books.

We may therefore conclude that the Ignatian chapter, clearly a Nativity passage, in all likelihood reflects Wisdom 18:14–15, which was already employed in some manner in the liturgy of Christmas.[38] If that conclusion is valid, then some kind of observance of Christmas developed much sooner than is usually supposed[39] and the liturgical Proper of Time was well advanced even in very early pre-Nicene days.

6

Christmas Echoes
at Paschaltide

In one of the oldest strata of Gospel tradition and within the brief compass of three verses (Mark 15:43, 46f.), there is an intriguing possibility that we have in the account of Christ's entombment an echo of His birth-story. There is present a man named Joseph ("from Arimathaea"), a Corpse wrapped in linen and laid *(katetheken)* in a tomb, and two women named Mary (one, the Magdalene; the other, mother of another Joseph). Similarly in Luke 2:4f., 7, there is still another Joseph ("of the city of Nazareth"), a newborn Baby wrapped in swaddling-clothes and laid *(aneklinen)* in a manger, and a Mary (Miriam) betrothed to this Joseph.

Other resemblances occur throughout the Passion-story. The last phrase of *Benedictus qui venit, "hosanna en tois hupsistois"* (Mark 11:10), recalls the opening words of *Gloria in excelsis, "doxa en hupsistois theoi"* (Luke 2:14). Christ's presence in the Temple immediately after His triumphal entry and on the next day (Mark 11:11, 15–19) evokes the account of His presentation in the Temple on the fortieth day and at the age of twelve (Luke 2:22–38, 41–49), especially since both passages mention the pigeons (Mark 11:15; Luke 2:24). The question of tribute to Caesar and the Lord's answer (Mark 12:14–17) remind one of Caesar's census decree at the beginning of Jesus's earthly life and His conformity to it (Luke 2:1–7). The discussion respecting the relation of Messiah to David (Mark 12:35–37) is presumably associated with the existence of genealogies purporting to trace the ancestry of Jesus in the Davidic line (Luke 3:23–38; cf. Matthew 1:2–16).

The charge by the servant girl that the Apostle Peter had been with Jesus "the Nazarene" (Mark 14:67) is one of the four such uses of that designation in Mark (cf. 1:24; 10:47; 16:6), but it also invites comparison with a statement in the Nativity tradition, "He shall be called a Nazorean" (Matthew 2:23), an unidentifiable citation of "the prophets." Much more striking, however, is the description of Christ, often repeated in the Passion pericopes, as "king of the Jews" (Mark 15:2, 9, 12, 18, 26; cf. 15:32). Here one inevitably thinks of the question of the Magi, "Where is the One who is born king of the Jews?" (Matthew 2:2). Finally there is the centurion's testimony after Christ's death, "Truly this man was God's Son" (Mark 15:39), recalling again the genealogy wherein the lineage of Christ is traced back to God (Luke 3:38).

In addition to these rather important likenesses are several less significant ones. For example, in the cynical Sadducean tale about a woman taken in leviratical marriage by her deceased husband's six brothers one after another (Mark 12:20–23), the mocking query, "Whose wife will she be?" must surely arouse recollections of the circumstances surrounding the relation of Joseph and Mary and Christ's birth (cf. Luke 1:34; Matthew 1:19). The account of the widow's mites (Mark 12:41–44) has affinities with the poor offering of the Blessed Virgin at the purification (Luke 2:24). There is moreover a distant possibility that the variant on the "parable of the talents" (Mark 13:33–37), the anointing in Bethany (Mark 14:3–9), and the offer of myrrh at the crucifixion (Mark 15:23) echo the threefold gift of the Magi in the birth-story (Matthew 2:11).

If these similarities are worthy of note, there can be three theories accounting for them. The first is coincidence; the second, an influence of the Passion stories on the Nativity tradition; and the third, an influence of the Nativity tradition on the Passion stories. The first is not likely, for mere chance seems to be excluded by the number of resemblances as well as by the sequence in which they occur. The second implies priority of the Passion record, as indeed the third implies it of the Nativity pericopes. Here, then, is the problem. No scholar doubts the genuine antiquity of the Passion narrative, originally as blocks of oral material long before the first Evangelist "took pen in hand" and perhaps, at least in part, as written material before that event. In general, therefore, these Passion pericopes could date from almost any period between A.D. 30 and 70.

The birth-stories in Luke 1 and 2, only loosely attached to that Gospel, are also very primitive. Their weighty Semitic quality is almost universally recognized and is evidence of early date. Part of them may be pre-Christian, part may be from a circle or sect venerating John the Baptizer, part may be Christian imitations of the Baptist cycle, and part may be local stories about Jesus, Christian from the beginning. Of these four possibilities, only the first and the last are truly relevant, for the second, the idea of a Baptist literature, is discredited and with it the third possibility vanishes.[1] The presence of pagan influence is possible but remote; the strong Jewishness of the language and circumstances precludes an immediate influence. It remains true, of course, that pre-Christian Judaism had already felt that influence.

In the nature of things the Passion pericopes obviously originated at a time after the date of the Crucifixion. If the Nativity narratives are of pre-Christian origin, they are equally obviously much earlier. On the other hand, if the birth-stories were based on local accounts about Jesus, they reflect no trace of His sufferings, not even the more artful Matthaean version. (One slight exception may exist in Luke 2:35a, but the allusion is so general as to be negligible.) Thus the pericopes incorporated into Matthew 1 and 2 and Luke 1 and 2—whether of pre-Christian or Christian origin—are necessarily older than the Passion stories. Any influence must therefore be by the former upon the latter rather than vice versa. There is in consequence an echoing of Christmas at Paschaltide, not the anachronistic reading of the Passion into the Christmas cycle.[2]

7

The Harrowing of Hell, Psalm 24,

and Pliny the Younger:

A Note

As late as the fifteenth century a prominent theme in medieval English prose and poetry was one usually called the "harrowing of hell." [1] Antecedents of it in Insular, as well as in Continental, literature are too numerous and familiar to cite at length. The motif is derived, mediately or immediately, from an apocryphal work known as the Gospel of Nicodemus or the Acts of Pilate. The latter part of the ancient document is an account of the descent of Christ into Hades, a narrative apparently older than the rest of the tale; actually of unknown date, it may have originated in the third or even second century. [2] The central idea, rescue of pre-Christian faithful believers from the hold of Hades, is still older and probably Scriptural (I Peter 3:19; 4:6). But there is a detail in many versions of the *descensus* that cannot be traced in any writing earlier than the Gospel of Nicodemus: when the Lord dies on the cross and goes to the place of departed spirits, He challenges the entrance to the nether region with the words (numerous variations) of

Psalm 24, "Lift up your heads, O gates! and be lifted up, O ancient doors! that the King of glory may come in." (The remaining verses are also usually incorporated into the story.)

The question may arise, How did this particular Psalm become associated with the "harrowing of hell"? Its appropriateness has been recognized not only in the literary sphere but also in liturgical and musical circles. It was appointed in the Divine Office, almost from the beginning, as a Proper Psalm for Holy Saturday Matins; and George Frederick Handel's immortal music has wedded it irrevocably to the interval between the tenor recitative of Good Friday, "He was cut off from the land of the living," and the bass air of Easter, "Thou art gone up on high." It is not impossible to reconstruct the process by which its propriety was noted.

In a remarkably short time after the days of Christ, His followers came to look upon His death not as defeat, but as victory. Indeed, according to tradition, Saint Peter, in a public statement about seven weeks after the crucifixion, applied to the Lord a passage from the sixteenth Psalm to the effect that Christ had conquered the fell grip of death (Acts 2:25–28). A similar sentiment was later attributed to Saint Paul (Acts 13:35–37). Soon, moreover, the church developed the corollary belief that Christ's death was not His victory only, but also the victory of all believers, the Lord being simply "the firstborn from the dead" or "the first-fruits of them that slept." [3] Once more they confirmed their conviction with suitable texts from the Old Testament, such as "O death, I will be thy plagues" and "Death is swallowed up for ever." [4]

At this point, however, some early disciple asked a sobering but filial question, "What happens to our fathers who died before Christ and the institution of His sacraments?"

Such a query seems to lie behind the Pauline reference to
Baptism for the dead (I Corinthians 15:29). For a brief
moment the infant church hesitated. But only for a moment,
for among the accounts afloat about the dreadful day of
crucifixion was one relating how the Lord assured the peni-
tent thief (Dysmas) a place that very day with Him in the
spirit-world, a place called Paradise (Luke 23:43)—the word
itself recalled Eden and the first parents of the race (Genesis
2:8; LXX). But there was another story far more dramatic,
namely, that at the instant of Christ's death, during the
mighty upheaval that accompanied it, many tombs were
opened and a number of the holy ones of former years came
back to life and wandered about the city of Jerusalem
(Matthew 27:52f.). Perhaps also certain Old Testament
passages came to reassure those who were wondering about
their beloved dead, such a passage, for example, as that one
about the Lord's bringing prisoners out of the dungeon and
those who sit in darkness out of the prison-house.[5]

It is easy enough to set an exact point for the rescue of the
pre-Christian righteous ones. Logically the only time the
harrowing could have taken place was during the interval
between the Lord's death and His resurrection: the other
stages of His life were accounted for by the forty days of
Resurrection-appearances followed by His glorious return
to the Father's right hand on high. When speculation had
reached this conclusion, the doctrine of the "harrowing of
hell" was complete in principle; elaboration only remained
and that rapidly followed.

Old Testament allusions to Sheol or place of the departed,
freighted with sad memories of Babylonian exile, inevitably
colored Christian speculation. As noted above, it was deemed
to be a place of shades and gloom, a dungeon-pit and a
prison.[6] It was moreover a place of silence, or rather of

croaking whispers, of faint, almost voiceless, chirping.[7] So somber indeed was the prospect that one of the ancient Psalmists, facing the approach of death, pleaded for a brief respite in which he could smile again before he was no more (Psalm 39:13).

On a number of details the traditional testimony, being ambiguous, allowed for creative and imaginative treatment by the early Christians. For instance, some Old Testament authors believed that in the world of the departed there was no differentiation of the good and bad, between the righteous and unrighteous;[8] others believed that a distinction of some sort did exist.[9] There were those who affirmed that it was a world of no return[10] and those who asserted, however vaguely, that the dead would live again.[11] Part of the tradition taught that it was a world apart from God, forgotten by Him (Job 7:8–10), while other portions suggested that Sheol was still within God's world and was not neglected by Him.[12] All these speculations, of course, recall pagan theories of the world of the dead.

Whatever these texts meant to their authors, to the minds of the early Christians they had significance in terms of the great revelation made by Christ. If the land of the dear departed was a place of gloomy shadows, a prison-dungeon of somber silence or of low, sibilant whispers; if it was a place of no return for all alike, whether good or bad, and hidden from the presence of God; and if it was the place that the Lord invaded victoriously between His cruel death and His mighty resurrection, then His visit there was a successful and triumphant raid, a veritable harrowing, which "brought life and immortality to light" and which was not overcome by the darkness;[13] which broke in sunder the bonds holding "the spirits in prison";[14] which brought the piercing, joyful sound of a trumpet-blast to the dismal quietness of the grave;[15] which wrought a clear distinction between the condition of the pious dead and the impenitent dead;[16] which proved that the power of death was abolished and that the dead would live again;[17] and which above all exemplified God's dominion over the world of the departed as well as over the realm of the living.[18]

In such a way as this we may reconstruct the evolution of the doctrine of the *descensus* and its meaning to Christians about the end of the first century, but we have not yet considered the association of Psalm 24 with the speculation. To that we now turn. On the cross the Lord was reputed to have begun the recitation of Psalm 22; it is conceivable that a devout believer might well have added the next two Psalms to his own meditation on his Master's death—they are certainly appropriate for that purpose—and thus have come habitually to think not upon the mournful words of Psalm 22, but upon the pleasanter sentiments of Psalm 23 and the challenging phrases of Psalm 24, as more expressive of the victory over death.

Another external circumstance may have had even weightier significance. Most of the earlier disciples were Jewish and remained quite loyal to Mosaic institutions: they did not quickly realize a discrepancy in adhering to the new belief and in attending the liturgy of the elder faith. It would be extremely surprising if they were unaware that the twenty-fourth Psalm was the Proper Psalm appointed in the Levitical ceremony for the first day of the week,[19] the very day on which the Lord had returned from the conquest of hell and death. They may often have heard it solemnly intoned in the Jerusalem Temple or in synagogues where they continued to worship for a long time. It is faintly, faintly possible that some of the grief-stricken Apostles had heard it in the Temple on that first Easter morning before the women hastened to them with the marvelous news of an empty tomb.

Devoted as the early Christians were both to their Master and to the Jewish liturgy, association of the Psalm with the Lord was well-nigh unavoidable, especially when further consideration was taken of the precise language of the Psalm. Perhaps the first word to strike a responsive chord in the Christian mind was "gates," twice repeated in the passage. Part of the conception of Hades or Sheol in the Old Testament was that of a walled city guarded by gates of brass.[20] That idea had already appeared in Christianity: in the tradition of Christ's giving the keys to Saint Peter, the Master had affirmed that "the gates of Hades" would not be able to resist the church's assault on the domain of death (Matthew 16:18). Moreover, about the turn of the century, a Christian writer had described Christ Himself as holding in His hands the keys of (the gates of) death and hell Revelation 1:18).

Perhaps the next word in the concatenation of ideas was "glory," also twice repeated in the Psalm in the phrase "King of glory." The Glory was the Shekinah, the blazing light that had descended upon the wilderness Tabernacle and Solomon's Temple,[21] the symbol of the Presence of God Himself. The real Shekinah had, of course, long since disappeared, but it was represented by everburning lamps, and a legend was still perpetuated that the Glory yet shone between the cherubim over the ark of the covenant in the Holy of Holies. Christians, however, dramatically identified their Lord with the Shekinah (James 2:1, Greek). Hence the phrase, "King of glory," was an apt allusion, as they no doubt assumed, to their Master as He launched His raid against "the gates of hell." Furthermore, if Christ was a mighty Ruler, characterized by dazzling brilliance, attacking a gloomy, fortified city, the city itself was obviously enemy-held or it would not make even a show of resistance. That thought appears in the Septuagint version of the Psalm (known to the Apostles and early Christians): "Lift up your gates, O princes." The word "princes" *(archontes)* is therefore the third one in the chain of associated ideas. To the primitive disciples the Greek form of this word, in the singular or plural, was used frequently to refer to Satan and his myrmidons.[22]

The paralleling of ideas embodied in the *descensus* doctrine with the phraseology of Psalm 24 seems to be fulfilled in two Pauline passages. The first text is I Corinthians 2:8, where the Apostle states that if "the princes of this age" had known the mystery of the wisdom of God (summarized later as the death, burial, and resurrection of Christ, cf. I Corinthians 15:3f.), they would not have crucified "the Lord of glory." Apart from James 2:1, this New Testament verse is the only verbal identification of Christ with the Shekinah: it seems to be a very strong reminiscence of the Psalmist's "King of glory" (a phrase which interestingly enough appears nowhere else in the Old Testament). The thought is that the powers of darkness unwittingly compassed their own defeat by what they supposed was their success in destroying Christ. The portrayal of the spoliation of the rulers of darkness appears even more vividly in a second text, Colossians 2:15, where Christ is said to have displayed them as captives in a public triumphal procession. With these two verses the association seems to be complete. I think we may therefore venture to assume, even without literary evidence and long before the preparation of the *descensus* section of the Gospel of Nicodemus, that the early Christian church was using the twenty-fourth Psalm liturgically to commemorate the Lord's victorious conquest of Hades and death.

If the foregoing conclusion is proximate to the truth, we may be able to cite a possible illustration of ceremonial use of Psalm 24 in Christian worship. The reference is, of course, the well-known letter of Pliny the Younger to Emperor Trajan about the middle of A.D. 113. The letter is exceedingly problematic, and the evidence it affords, although fairly extensive, is quite vague. Pliny was a Roman official, contemptuous of the new "superstition," but somewhat alarmed by its growth. His information was derived from Christian deserters, one of whom had apostatized as early as A.D. 93. According to them, Pliny reported, Christians were essentially harmless, the height of their folly being that they had a regular practice of gathering before dawn on a fixed day, at which time they were accustomed to utter in an antiphonal manner *(dicere secum invicem)* a *carmen* to Christ as to a god, as well as to bind themselves in a solemn way *(sacramento)* not to commit thefts, robberies, or adulteries, not to break faith, nor to violate a trust. Later, on the same day, they reassembled for an innocuous common meal.[23]

Not dismissing the ambiguity of the passage, let us see what it yields in terms of our previous conjecture. There are several points to be observed. First, I think we may quite plausibly assume without debate that the "fixed day" was a Sunday. Less plausibly, we may suppose that it was an Easter Sunday: the statement concerning an assembly before dawn may imply the night-vigil preceding Easter. And we remember that Psalm 24, the Proper Psalm for Sunday in Jewish worship, was now presumably associated by the Christians with Christ's conquest of death. Secondly, the word *carmen* and its many shades of meaning are noteworthy. It means

verse as opposed to prose and the melody; it is usually re-
stricted to lyric and epic as distinct from dramatic verse;
and it may mean a religious formula or an oracular prophecy.
I suggest that here it means a *Psalm* as opposed to a *hymn* or
a *spiritual song*.[24]

Thirdly, identification of the twenty-fourth Psalm is still
further intimated by Pliny. It was uttered (sung?) *anti-
phonally:* the most striking and colorful features of Psalm
24 are the thrilling challenges and answers of verses 7–10.
It is sung "to Christ as to a god": Psalm 24 corresponds to
that description, as we have observed earlier, in the identification of Christ with the Glory. Even more interesting,
however, is Pliny's reference to the oath by which Christians
bound themselves: four details are mentioned, thievery (and
banditry), adultery, lying, and violation of trust.[25] It is precisely those four points which are enumerated in verse 4 of
the Psalm as characterizing the man who may stand in the
Lord's holy place and receive a blessing: he must be a man
of clean hands (not soiled with stolen goods) and a pure
heart (who has not looked with lustful eyes upon a woman),[26] a man who has not lifted up his soul to falsehood and
who has not sworn deceitfully though it were to his own
hurt.[27]

My analysis of Pliny's letter is, of course, by no means
certain; it is, I hope, significant and suggestive. But, as intimated earlier, we do not find absolutely clear literary evidence of the association of Psalm 24 with Christ's descent
into hell until we reach the *descensus* portion of the Gospel
of Nicodemus. By that time, however, the treatment is so
elaborate that we must apparently assume such a development as has been described. Most of the Old Testament texts
to which I have alluded are cited in full and in dramatic
fashion in the Nicodemus account. The story is rich and

imaginative and it has become a part of the literary, liturgical, and musical heritage of Western civilization.

It should be noted that use of the Psalm was extended to
other occasions, particularly to the festival of Ascension and
to the service for dedication or consecration of a church.[28]
But these usages are not really different from celebration of
the conquest of Hades and death. As Dom Gregory Dix has
shown, the Paschal observance of the pre-Nicene church
commemorated the entire complex of beliefs connected with
Easter (the Harrowing, Resurrection, and Ascension); only
later were these ideas separated and assigned to other appropriate dates.[29] Moreover, the dedication of a church also
contains the concept of a conquest of the sphere of darkness
and the transfer of its ownership or occupancy to the Lord
of glory.[30] As a matter of fact, the extended application of
Psalm 24 might be interpreted as partial evidence that the
Psalm was already established as a feature of the liturgy of
Christ's victory over hell.

8

Petronius
and the Gospel
before the Gospels?

a. A Footnote to the "Petronian Question"

Recently while reviewing the *Satiricon* of Petronius
for casual entertainment only, I was suddenly impressed by
a series of minor, but nonetheless tantalizing, resemblances
between the famous Milesian tale of the matron of Ephesus
and Biblical accounts of the burial of Christ.[1] The scene is
laid in a cemetery and a vault-tomb *(conditorium, hypo-
gaeum, monumentum, casula)* near a place of execution,
where the crucifixion of several criminals had just been accomplished.[2] The victims, condemned as robbers *(latrones)*,
had been sentenced to death by the governor of the province *(imperator provinciae)*.[3] At the respectable sepulcher
of a deceased Ephesian gentleman, two women (his widow
and one of her slaves) had been keeping mournful vigil night
and day for five days.[4] By the crosses a young soldier was
stationed to prevent theft of the corpses for decent inter-
ment.[5]

During the ensuing night (the fifth for the weeping wom-

en) the soldier saw a light among the tombs and heard the
sound of lamentation.[6] Piqued by curiosity he decided to
investigate. At first sight of the beautiful matron, he was
frightened by dread of a supernatural apparition, but his
fears were soon allayed.[7] He was shortly able to persuade
both women to partake of food and to prevail on the widow
to yield to his charms. That night and the two following, he
and she, with connivance of the servant, kept their shameless
assignation in the vault without detection.

In the meanwhile, the parents of one of the crucified
criminals had observed that watch was being negligently
kept. Awaiting their opportunity, they had, on the fourth
night after the execution, stolen their's son's corpse from a
cross and buried it in secret.[8] Early the next morning the
soldier discovered the theft and, fully expecting just punishment for dereliction of duty, prepared to end his life with
his own sword.[9] The quick-witted widow, however,
shrewdly suggested that her husband's body be affixed to
the empty cross. The deed was speedily effected; the government had its required number of crucified victims; and
the people of the city marveled that a dead man had mounted
the cross.

These coincidences, of course, demanded closer inspection, and immediately at hand were three additional details,
again minor but intriguing. The cynical story had been told
by Eumolpus, on the eve of a storm at sea, to shame a notorious Levantine courtesan named Tryphaena, who was on
her way into banishment. Amid general hilarity at the end
of the narrative, she showed unexpectedly that she had rem-
nants of a sense of honor by blushing deeply at this tale of
woman's faithlessness. We recall that among the members
of the Christian church in Rome whom Saint Paul greeted,
there was a worker by the name of Tryphaena.[10] Furthermore, the locale was Ephesus, an early scene of Pauline ac-

tivity and at a later date presumably the see of the Apostle John. Finally, the nine-day interval in the story is very faintly reminiscent of a similar lapse of time between the ascension of Christ and the Pentecostal outpouring of the Holy Spirit.[11]

A question now presents itself: "Do these vague similarities have any real significance?" To which we must truthfully reply: "Perhaps not." Yet in all justice we shall add, tentatively and as an afterthought: "But possibly so." We admit that there seem to be no resemblances in the *Satiricon* other than those in the matron of Ephesus story.[12] Shortly before that tale, there is a single reference to the Jewish rite of circumcision, but information about that practice was widespread among Roman writers and would require no special competence in Palestinian matters.[13] One of the poems attributed to Petronius may suggest a little more knowledge: in it occurs not only the inevitable mention of circumcision, but also of the *herem* (ban or excommunication), holy city (Jerusalem), sabbath, and law of fasting. In it also the author deduces from the dietary tabu against pork that the Jewish object of worship was a totemic pig-god.[14] (I append these Jewish notices because Judaism and Christianity were imperfectly distinguished by outsiders at first; indeed it was not until the second century that the Romans became aware of the absolute differentiation.)[15]

The preceding remarks are only a summary of evidence[16] (if we may use so strong a term) found in a critical edition of the text of Petronius. Surely now the commentators will give us full explication. But when we turn to them we are confronted not only with a bewildering number of Petronian studies (one book devoted exclusively to a bibliography of such treatises), but also, and above all, with an apparently insoluble "Petronian question" (that is, identification and date of the author of the *Satiricon*).[17] General opinion has hitherto favored the Petronius (died A.D. 66)—Nero's *elegantiae arbiter*—mentioned by Tacitus in his *Annals*,[18] but of late there is a growing suspicion that the author was another Petronius of the late Antonine period (after 180).[19]

If, on one hand, we assume the later date for our Petronius, and if we also attach serious import to the resemblances here noted, then the following data are pertinent. Even by consent of the most liberal scholarship, all four canonical Gospels had been in circulation for at least half a century. Christian apologists were already at work clarifying and explaining their religion for the imperial authorities. Distinction between Judaism and Christianity was fully comprehended by the government.[20] The Pauline saga was sufficiently well known to have evoked an influential heresy (Marcionism) and a fictional romance (the *Acts of Paul*, in which incidentally an Asia Minor queen named Tryphaena plays a prominent role).[21] Christianity, as well as the mysteries, was definitely "in the air"; and the story of the faithless widow was already current in a literary treatment by Phaedrus.[22] At the later date, therefore, we can with no difficulty account for the coincidences, if indeed they are significant. But we face another challenge: "Why, then, are not the resemblances clearer and more positive?" To that we can give no answer except to remind the inquirer of the fragmentary condition of Petronius and to suggest that more evident allusions may have appeared in certain passages no longer preserved. Or we may intimate that Petronius was in no way interested in Christian stories.

If, on the other hand, we assume the Neronian Petronius as author of the *Satiricon*, and if we still attach importance to the alleged similarities we have observed, then we are dealing with a date at which, except on the most conservative criticism, no canonical Gospel had been composed. Pauline activity, however, had already been extensive (the Apostle died *ca.* 67). The Roman government knew about Christianity and Judaism, but had only the vaguest notion of the difference between the two religions, a notion shared by many Christians and Jews of mid-first century.[23] And as far as we know, the Phaedrian account of the Ephesian widow story had been published only a short time before. If this earlier period is the date of the Petronian novel, we shall less easily explain the apparent coincidences, supposing that they are not accidental.

Yet the supposition itself is far more reasonable on the basis of a first-century date. The very vagueness of the similarities can be understood if Petronius' information was derived from hearsay. The atmosphere of gossip is quite obvious in the Tacitus account of Christianity in Rome in those years and is confirmed by the Matthean record of a story spread abroad by the Jews about the theft of a body.[24] The statement by Tacitus that Christ was crucified by order of the procurator, Pontius Pilate, throws light on Petronius' phrase, *imperator provinciae* (which seems to be crux of the commentators), especially in view also of the Biblical use of the same term to characterize both the Emperor Tiberius and his minor official in Judaea.[25] In fact, using the earlier date, we can quite plausibly imagine Petronius picking up from a migrant stock of stories the Milesian tale and embellishing it cynically with tags from a garbled oral version of an equally improbable report about a new god.[26] The speculation is even more plausible if the poem referred to earlier is correctly attributed to him: in that case we know that he had considerable, if inaccurate, information about several religious observances emanating from Pales-

tine; and still more, if we can depend on Tacitus' assertion
that Petronius had served as proconsul in Bithynia.[27] Christianity had already entered that province of Asia Minor by
the middle of the first century;[28] and it was there a half-
century later that we find, however problematic, our fullest
early literary account of Christianity from a pagan source,
indeed from the pen of another notable proconsul.[29]

In the final analysis, of course, the preceding speculations,
highly conjectual and tentative as they are, do not conclu-
sively prove anything. They do no more than add a modest
footnote to the "Petronian question" (my sole intention, as
my title intimates) and suggest, I hope, another facet of this
many-faceted problem.[30]

b. The *Satiricon* and the Christian Oral Tradition

Several years ago I offered a tentative suggestion that some
"minor, but nonetheless tantalizing, resemblances between
the famous Milesian tale of the matron of Ephesus" in the
Satiricon and the Biblical account of Christ's burial were the
result of cynical and garbled use by Petronius of an oral
version of the new Christian gospel that he may have heard,
perhaps in Bithynia.[1] So modest was my proposal that I supposed there were no other resemblances. I now believe, however, that at several other points the oral version of the
Christian tradition impinges upon Petronius' picaresque romance.

There are a few details of his life[2] to which I wish first to
direct attention, since they apparently lend credence to the
possibility and even probability of this influence. In A.D. 39,
when Petronius was only nineteen or twenty years old, he
accompanied his uncle, Publius, when that kinsman became

governor of the province of Syria. For a while he may have enjoyed the life of Antioch-on-the-Orontes, as well as a visit to Egypt.

It is well then to remember that he was in Palestine at the very time when the new religion movement was creating its initial stir in legal trials and persecutions. It was indeed in Antioch about this very time that "Christians" first received that appellation (Acts 11:26). And Saint Paul had visited there about 38.[3] The governor, Publius Petronius, was indeed indirectly involved in these affairs. It was he whom Caligula ordered to install the imperial image in the Temple at Jerusalem and it was in the summer of 40 that he advanced to obey the order. This particular effort caused such dismay among both Jews and Christians that its effect can still be read in the pages of the New Testament (cf. Mark 13:14). Because Publius Petronius realized its folly, he delayed and tried to dissuade the emperor. The latter, infuriated at such an attitude, decreed the governor's suicide, but the execution was not accomplished, for Caligula himself was assassinated on 24 January 41.[4]

If within the years 40–42 young Petronius traveled anywhere in the eastern Mediterranean area he would have inevitably seen and heard about the new movement. And when he did become governor of Bithynia in 55–56, he was in an area where the Christian mission was unusually successful.[5] It was probably while he was in Bithynia, about 56, that Saint Paul was enduring his Caesarean imprisonment under the governor Felix. What is of interest is the apparent association of Felix's wife Drusilla in the government (Acts 24:24). Her name would have a familiar ring to Petronius because it was the same as that of Emperor Caligula's sister, whose deification proceedings he had attended and ridiculed somewhat earlier.[6] All in all there is every reason to surmise that Petronius did in fact have ample opportunity to gain some knowledge of the Christian gospel while it was in its preliterary stage. It is a fact that his name or that of a member of his family (his uncle Publius? another?), remembered by Christians, entered the Christian tradition. For according to the apocryphal Gospel of Peter (*ca.* 150), viii, 31,[7] the centurion guarding Christ's sepulcher bears the name of Petronius.

I shall not again treat the story of the matron of Ephesus here, nor the mention by both Saint Paul and Petronius of a woman named Tryphaena,[8] but, contrary to my former statement, I now assert that the remark in *Satiricon* 74, "haec dicente eo gallus gallicinaceus cantavit," is significant in view of the identical sentiment and a number of similar words in Luke 22:60: "kai parachrema eti lalountos autou ephonesen alektor."

There are six other places where Biblical allusions spring immediately to mind. First, there is a statement near the end of *Satiricon* 63, that witches (mulieres plussciae . . . nocturnae) exist who "turn downward what is upward" (quod sursum est, deorsum faciunt). Similarly at Thessalonica the early Christians (who were also people of the nighttime)[9] were said (Acts 17:6), about 49 or 50, to be "those who upset the world" *(hoi ten oikoumenen anastatosantes).*

Secondly, near the beginning of *Satiricon* 75, Habinnas reminds Trimalchio that "we are men, not gods" (homines sumus, non dei). So about 46–49 Saint Paul at Lystra had to defend himself against divine worship as an apparition of Hermes by crying out (Acts 14:15), "We are indeed men like you" *(kai hemeis homoiopatheis esmen humin anthropoi).*

Third, toward the beginning of *Satiricon* 78 occurs a remark by Trimalchio of his graveclothes, "See to it, Stichus,

that neither mice nor moths touch them" (Vide tu . . . ,
Stiche, ne ista mures tangant aut tineae). Surely this is an
echo of the original which lies beneath Matthew 6:20, "but
lay up treasures for yourselves in heaven where neither moth
nor rust destroys" *(thesaurizete de humin thesaurous en
ouranoi hopou oute ses oute brosis aphanizei).*

Fourth, in the middle of *Satiricon* 105, it was decided
that to appease the guardian-deity of the ship "forty stripes
be inflicted on each one" (placuit quadragenas utrique plagas
imponi). Perhaps of no great significance, but, nonetheless,
the Apostle records (II Corinthians 11:24) that five times
he received from the Jews stripes to the number of "forty
less one" *(tesserakonta para mian).*

Fifth, the first line of a metrical passage in *Satiricon* 109
states: "Fallen are the hairs—that which alone is the glory
of the body" (Quod solum formae decus est, cecidere ca-
pilli). In like manner Saint Paul believed (I Corinthians
11:15) that for a woman her hair "is her glory" *(doxa autei
estin).* There is here also a faint reminiscence of the Lord's
declaration (Matthew 10:30), "Even the hairs of your head
are all numbered" *(humon de kai hai triches tes kephales
pasai erithmemenai eisin).*

Sixth, midway through *Satiricon* 131 an old woman performs a spell thus: "she soon took upon her middle finger
dust mixed with spittle and signed the forehead" (mox tur-
batum sputo pulverem medio sustulit digito frontemque . . .
signavit) of a man who protested all the while. So when
Christ healed the blind man at the pool of Siloam (John 9:6),
"He spat upon the ground and made clay out of the spittle,
and put the clay upon his eyes" *(eptusen chamai kai epoiesen
pelon ek tou ptusmatos kai epetheken autou ton pelon epi
tous ophthalmous).* This is, of course, a folk-pattern that can
be frequently discovered.

In addition to these six points we may also add a certain cynical commendation of celibacy (qui vero nec uxores unquam duxerunt . . . ad summos honores perveniunt, id est soli militates, soli fortissimi atque etiam innocentes habentur [*Satiricon* 116, *ad fin.*]), which agrees in part with some tendencies in primitive Christianity. And we should perhaps also add the account of the shipwreck (*Satiricon* 113–115), which in many ways parallels the account of Saint Paul's adventures in Acts 27.

Let us admit that each of these points singly is not very impressive, but the cumulative effect is quite strong. To me it seems apparent that Petronius had heard some oral versions of the Christian message and mission and that he employed many words, phrases, and situations from it to give a certain piquant flavor to his romance.

c. The Matron of Ephesus Again: An Analysis

Christopher Fry was "discovered" in 1946 when his comedy *A Phoenix too Frequent* appeared. Since that time the play has gone through no less than nine printings, the latest being in 1959, indicating a degree of interest and popularity. Fry states on one of the earlier pages of his book that "The story was got from Jeremy Taylor who had it from Petronius." On turning back to the good bishop we find a version of the story near the very end of his *Holy Living and Dying*, correctly attributed to Petronius.[1] It would appear that Fry knew only the version in Taylor and nothing directly from the one in Petronius, for he follows the former in describing the mode of execution as hanging, not crucifixion as in the latter.

The incident, commonly called "the matron of Ephesus" or "the faithless widow" story, has had an extensive history, both in Latin and in the vernaculars. Far better than the somewhat romanticized account of Bishop Taylor is one that appears in the writings of another Englishman, indeed of another prelate, John of Salisbury, bishop of Chartres. In the eighth book of his *Policraticus* he related the tale from Petronius almost *verbatim*, following it with the statement that for whatever it was worth Flavian vouched for the historicity of the incident.[2]

The story has attracted much scholarly, as well as popular, attention and inevitably the search for sources and analogues has been persistent.[3] As far as is certainly known, it appeared first in the writings credited to Phaedrus (*ca.* 15 B.C.–A.D. 50),[4] but the most familiar version is obviously the one by Petronius (*ca.* A.D. 19–*ca.* 66), embedded in his inimitable *Satiricon*.[5] And it has been generally assumed that the latter derived it from the former. That may indeed be true, but it is equally possible, if the event described were an actual occurrence, that Phaedrus and Petronius were both independently giving literary form to a notorious incident.

In order to have the data before us, both stories are here presented in translation as literal as English idiom will permit. First, Phaedrus:

> Not many years ago a certain woman lost a beloved husband and laid his body in a tomb. Since she could not be torn away from it, but was determined to spend her life mourning in the sepulcher, she gained the illustrious reputation of a chaste virgin.
>
> In the meanwhile men who had pillaged a temple of Jupiter had paid the penalties to divine majesty by suffering crucifixion. That no one could take away their remains, soldiers are furnished as guards of the corpses where the woman had confined herself.
>
> On this occasion one of the guards, becoming thirsty, asked water of a young slave girl at midnight. She was, it

happens, attending her mistress who was then preparing to go to sleep, for she had worked at night and had prolonged her vigils until a late hour.

Since the gates were opened a little, the soldier peers in and sees an extraordinary woman of beautiful face. His heart, instantly arrested, is enkindled and a passion of uncontrollable emotion consumes him. Adroit keenness finds a thousand reasons by which he might see her more often. Overcome by the daily habit, she is little by little made more submissive to the stranger, and soon a closer tie has bound her heart.

While the attentive guard passes the night here, a body was stolen from one cross. The troubled soldier revealed the deed to the woman. But the holy virgin says, "It is not what you fear," and she hands over her husband's body to be affixed to the cross, that the soldier may not undergo the penalties of negligence. Thus shame took the place of praise.

The following is the account offered by Petronius:

A certain matron of Ephesus was of such notable virtue that she stirred the women of the neighboring communities for a sight of her. When therefore this woman was bearing her husband to the grave, she was not content in common fashion to follow the funeral procession with hair disheveled or to beat her naked breast before the eyes of the multitude. She indeed followed the deceased into the sepulcher and began to guard the body (which was placed in an underground crypt of Greek style) and to lament day and night. Injuring herself in this manner and striving for death by abstinence from food, neither parents nor kinsmen could entice her away. At length even the rebuffed magistrates withdrew.

The woman, a unique paragon, mourned by everyone, was already dragging out her fifth day without nourishment. Beside the ailing woman her very devoted maidservant was sitting, adding her tears to the grieving woman's and renewing the light placed in the tomb whenever it went out. Throughout the entire city there was one tale. Men of

every rank were avowing that this alone shone brilliantly as
a true example of virtue and love.

In the meanwhile the governor of the province ordered
robbers to be crucified near that little dwelling where the
matron was bewailing the fresh corpse. On the next night
when a soldier, who was guarding the crosses so that no
one might take the bodies down for burial, observed a light
shining very brightly among the tombs and heard the groan-
ing of weeping women, he longed, with the bad habit of
humankind, to know who or what was doing that. He went
down therefore into the sepulcher, but when he had observed such a beautiful woman he stopped immediately,
confused as though by a certain apparition, as by phantoms
of the lower regions.

As soon, however, as he saw the body of the dead man
and reflected upon the tears and the face scratched by
fingernails, he realized what it was, namely, that the woman could not bear her grief for the dead one. He brought
to the tomb his own little supper and undertook to urge the
mourning one not to persist in useless sorrow or to break
her heart with unavailing sigh, "for there is the same last
home and dwelling place for all men," and other sentiments
with which embittered minds are summoned back to right
reason. But ignoring consolation, she beat and lacerated her
breast more violently and, tearing out her tresses, laid them
on the dead man's breast.

The soldier, however, did not leave but strove with the
same urgency to give the young woman food, until the
maid-servant, enticed by the odor of the wine offered by
him, finally stretched out a vanquished hand to the kindly
allurer. Thereupon, refreshed by drink and food, she began
to attack her mistress's persistence and says, "What will it
profit you[6] if you are weakened by fasting, if you have
buried yourself alive, if you have poured out a spirit un-
condemned before the Fates demand? 'Do you believe that
ashes and the buried shades feel this?'" [Vergil, *Aeneid*, iv,
34].

"Do you want to come to life again? Feminine uncer-
tainty thrown aside, do you want to enjoy the advantages

of light as long as it shall be permitted? That very body of the dead man ought to warn you to live."

No one listens unwillingly when he is exhorted to take food and live. Consequently, the woman, wasted with several days' abstinence, suffered her resolution to be shattered and filled herself with food no less greedily than the maid who had been earlier overcome. For the rest, you know what commonly tempts a full human being. With the same blandishments with which the soldier had persuaded the matron to want to live, he now made advances on her virtue. To the chaste woman indeed he seemed a handsome and eloquent young man, with the maid pleading his cause and frequently reciting: "Will you fight against a pleasing love? Has it not entered your mind in whose ploughed lands you will station yourself?" [Vergil, *Aeneid*, iv, 38f.].

Why do I delay any further? The woman did not long withhold that part of her body and the triumphant soldier was doubly convincing. They slept together not only that one night in which they consummated the union but also the next day and the third day, of course with the doors of the sepulcher closed tightly so that if anyone known to them or a stranger had come to the tomb he would have thought that the very virtuous wife had perished over her husband's body.

The soldier, charmed by the woman's comeliness and by the secrecy, purchased whatever provisions he could with his means and brought them at nightfall to the tomb. And so it was that the parents of one of the crucified victims, when they perceived that custody was relaxed, took down their hanging son one night and buried him with the final rites.

When the outwitted soldier was resuming his place on the next day, he saw one cross without a corpse. Terrified he told the woman what punishment would befall him, and further that he would not await the magistrate's judgment but would himself pronounce sentence upon his slothfulness with his own sword. Would she grant him a place when he was dead and provide the fatal sepulcher for lover as well as for husband?

The woman, no less merciful than virtuous, replies, "The gods grant that I may not at the same time witness the funeral of the two men dearest to me! I would rather hang the dead than kill the living." In accordance with this utterance she orders the body of her husband to be taken from the casket and to be nailed to the cross which was empty. The soldier accomplished the scheme of the very clever woman and on the next day the people wondered how a dead man had mounted the cross.

In spite of differences to be noted, it is quite obvious that Phaedrus and Petronius are telling the same story, one involving the same three players (the matron, her maid, and the soldier). The devotion of the woman to her deceased husband is emphasized and her reputation for virtue is set forth. The vain attempt of the citizenry to dissuade her from dwelling in or near the tomb of her husband is a subject of both authors, and they agree about her beauty as well as her virtue. Both recount the crucifixions near the sepulcher and the need for guards. Both confirm her seduction by the soldier at nighttime and both relate the theft of a body from one of the crosses, as well as the woman's offer of her late husband's body as a substitute to save the guard from punishment.

There are, it is true, some ambiguities within both narratives. In Phaedrus' version a band of soldiers was set to guard the executed criminals. Apart from that brief statement, however, only one soldier was involved in the tale. If several had been present, surely they would not have left the place unguarded. But Phaedrus conveniently ignores his minor inconsistency, for otherwise he would have had no story at all. Petronius wisely mentions one guard only and thus avoids the difficulty. It is likely that Phaedrus' unwitting reference to a plurality of soldiers more accurately reflects actual practice on such occasions, but Petronius' method, although less credible historically, is certainly the more artistic. His employment of a single guard renders his version practically impossible as an actual occurrence, while Phaedrus' casual reference, suggesting as it does what was probably customary, makes his story artistically impossible. The obvious inference is that such a story never really happened, but that it was fabricated out of whole cloth merely for entertainment. Or, alternatively, that it did happen, but only once, uniquely, and thus became a *cause célèbre*.

The other ambiguity belongs to Petronius. Both authors stress the beauty of the widow in superlative terms and Phaedrus never suggests any change. Petronius, however, goes on to describe her as following the cortège with disheveled hair and breast exposed to view. Five days later, wasted with fasting, she was a woman with face tear-streaked and torn by fingernails, her breast violently lacerated, and large patches of her hair torn out by the roots. It seems curiously contradictory to state that a woman of such appearance was still beautiful. But Petronius was not troubled. In the nature of things his romance required a beautiful woman, so he ignored his ambiguity. It appears that Phaedrus' version is the more credible although less true to reality, while Petronius' account is artistically the better, although not likely to have been factually true. As in the instance of the ambiguity in Phaedrus, this Petronian one leads to the inference that the story is contrived, not based on any known actual happening, although in this later case there is a definite statement by the narrator, Eumolpus, that it "occurred within his own memory," [7] a commonplace among story-tellers which inspires no confidence in its historical veracity. Or which indeed may mean no more than that he had read or heard the Phaedrian account.

The basic identity of the stories as related by Phaedrus

and Petronius does not obscure their dissimilarities. Externally the former is poetry; the latter, prose. The former is told in 164 Latin words; the latter, in 604, being virtually four times the former in length. The former gives no indication of the scene of the action; the latter, with characteristic artistry, locates it in the great city of Ephesus. But such outward differences are as nothing when compared with the inner ones, most of which involve distinct improvements of the story.

These we may consider under four topics: the maid, the matron, the soldier, and the situation. We begin with the maid. In the Phaedrian fable she is quite incidental, appearing briefly and by chance *(forte)*, occupying only a single sentence, and serving no real purpose. But she is very important in the Petronian version, playing an integral part in the account. Devoted to her mistress, she was willing to share completely the heroine's fate as well as to perform the usual tasks falling to a servant. She is the first to succumb to the soldier's proffer of food and drink. She thereupon adds her pleas to the soldier's to persuade her mistress to eat and live. It was her words that finally prevailed. And then she aided the soldier to seduce the matron. Above all, she is not only efficient and effective, but also literate, quoting Vergil's *Aeneid* twice. The story indeed hangs on the part she plays. Phaedrus could have done without her, but Petronius could not.

The matron herself is also quite differently portrayed by the two authors. In Phaedrus her fame arose from her devotion to her deceased husband. She had determined to spend the remainder of her life by his tomb, keeping vigil indeed, but otherwise practicing no austerities. When the soldier began to pay attention to her, she was slow to respond. Over a prolonged period of time he invented occasions to see her and only "little by little" was her heart at last conquered by him. Petronius relates that the matron's fame was widespread even during her husband's lifetime, so notable indeed that women from the area came from miles around merely to catch sight of her. When her husband died, she decided to starve herself to death lamenting at his tomb. So prominent and well known was she that her parents and kindred besought her not to act thus, but to return to her home and live. Even the magistrates of Ephesus tried to use their authority with her but met with rebuff and finally left her there. During what would have been her last days, high and low, rich and poor alike mourned her and kept her name and reputation alive, relating the marvel to all passing strangers. Yet, astonishingly enough, this paragon of virtue yielded quickly. On the very night of the soldier's first appearance, she succumbed to his food and blandishments with only a token resistance.

But of the three people the soldier provides the most interesting difference in the two treatments. In Phaedrus he simply becomes thirsty and in the most natural manner asks the servant girl for some water. The whole proceeding is an act of chance. In Petronius, on the other hand, there is an element of suspense. The soldier saw a strange light amid the tombs and heard groans. His curiosity was piqued. And instead of his needing water, it was he in the Petronian account who brought food and drink to the weeping women. In Phaedrus the soldier was passionately smitten by the matron's beauty at first sight. In Petronius he reeled back in shock, surprise, confusion, fear of the supernatural, of an apparition from the nether world, before he finally recognized the true situation.

He is also portrayed differently in the dénouement of the stories. In Phaedrus the soldier was troubled by the theft of the body when he reported it to the matron. But in Petronius he was terrified. He frantically reported the doom that awaited him, announced his intention of suicide, and pleaded for the woman to grant him burial beside her late husband. Phaedrus laid the crime to obvious negligence, but Petronius, more subtly and more shrewdly, to listlessness or sloth.

Lastly, the circumstances of the story are presented in differing ways. There are no explicit references to time in the Phaedrian fable and few implicit ones. But the Petronian version offers a detailed time-scheme. It was on the fifth day of the woman's vigil that the crucifixion occurred. On the next, the sixth, night, the woman was seduced by the soldier. Assignations followed on the seventh and eighth nights. And it was apparently on the ninth night that a body was stolen from a cross.[8] In Phaedrus there is no hint of the supernatural, but in Petronius there is a fear of phantoms and apparitions. In Phaedrus the doors of the sepulcher were closed all the time, but in Petronius the doors were significantly closed only during the seduction. In Phaedrus the crucified criminals were guilty of sacrilege and profanation, of pillaging a temple of Jupiter. In Petronius they were guilty only of robbery or banditry. And at the very end Phaedrus provides a "moral": the woman now incurred shameful disgrace in place of her former praiseworthy reputation. But Petronius cynically and immorally remarks that cleverness prevailed and the stupid people of the city could only marvel.

Before passing on, it may be worthwhile to inquire whether it is proper to designate this story as "The Faithless Widow." [9] There is not the slightest suggestion in either Phaedrus or Petronius that the woman had ever been unfaithful to her husband while he was living. Since death severs the marriage bond, the matron as widow was under no further obligation to her late husband. The tale therefore is not of a faithless widow, but of a seduction, simple enough, unusual perhaps only in its surroundings, that is, in a place of burial. In reality the soldier accomplished a worthy end by immoral means. In the Petronian account it is obvious that the woman was bent upon suicide, which regardless of mid-first century Roman theory and practice is wrong. To save the matron from executing her purpose was therefore a good deed. And since he saved her life, it was only just, in the dénouement, for her to express gratitude by saving his life. One may and should admit that the means employed were not meritorious, but to save life and to express gratitude are not unworthy acts. It must be further admitted that the story is told quite cynically without conscious effort at moralism, but despite the cynicism of the authors the story does have its own moral application, albeit unintentional.

The woman was not a "faithless widow" or, if she was, she was faithless not to her husband but to herself and then only after a manner of speaking. All the so-called analogues are therefore irrelevant. One such is a rabbinic story. A rabbi, wanting to test his wife's fidelity, persuaded one of his students to arrange an assignation with her. But at the place and on the night appointed, the rabbi in disguise met his wife, made love to her, and spent the night with her. On arising the next morning the woman was so frightened when she discovered that the lover was her husband that she immediately committed suicide. It is perfectly clear that there is no relation between that story and the Latin one. The most elaborate analogue discussed by Eduard Grisebach is the one entitled "The Matron of the Land of Sung," related in Remusat's *Contes chinois*.[10] But once again the parallel fails. The chief person in the Chinese (or Chinese-Indian) story is a philosopher, not the woman. It is a test case like the rabbinic tale, not a supposedly real and natural occurrence. The only true correspondence lies in a statement, "A sepulcher is at last the eternal home of all men," which is similar to the quotation in Petronius, "There is the same last home and dwelling place for all men." It is quite possible, however, that the French compiler was there influenced by the Petronian narrative. It seems to me almost incredible that this Chinese account should have ever been deemed a counterpart of the Latin story. The arbitrary designation as "the faithless widow" has probably been the misleading element.

These are only two illustrations, but there is similarly no relation between the Latin account and any of the other supposed analogues collected by Grisebach. It therefore remains that the Latin story was invented by Phaedrus and elaborated by Petronius. Thence it passed into world literature and eventually into folk tales. Or, as noted earlier, it was the record of a real and unique incident that was notorious enough to be remembered and reduced to writing by them. It follows, then, that despite the folkloristic sound of Eumolpus' remark that he would relate a true event that happened within his memory, the narrator was probably speaking the truth (that is, about the incident itself or about his reading of it in Phaedrus).

What has been quite remarkable is the discovery of close parallels at many points to Christian sources. Detailed verbal relationships have been discussed elsewhere.[11] Here we glance for a moment at the overall picture, for there is in the Latin versions a faint undertone of the Christian (or Jewish-Christian) doctrine of vicarious atonement. Farfetched as it may seem, here is an instance in which a crucified body saved another man's life. There is still further an intimation of either the ancient Jewish canard about the disappearing body of Christ[12] or of the Docetic heresy that only a phantom appeared to die on the cross. One can hardly avoid the impression, at least in the Petronian form, that the Christian gospel is reflected, however dimly and however perversely, in the entire story as well as in specific details.

We may summarize as follows. The story is definitely not folklore. Possibly such an incident occurred in the first century A.D. and was reduced to verse by Phaedrus. Petronius either knew of the occurrence by hearsay or knew of Phaedrus' account. In any case he elaborated it for his mocking novel by a more artistic treatment, in the course of which he made use of suggestions from Christian sources. It is just likely that it was a subconscious awareness of Christian elements that gave the story its long life in Western literature.

d. The Matron of Ephesus: An Identification

If one forgets most of the particularities of the "matron of Ephesus" tale as related by Phaedrus and Petronius,[1] he discovers a narrative divided roughly into three parts. The first is an account or description of a widow famed for her chastity and even called a virgin, but who is ultimately seduced by a soldier. The second is a gruesome story of a substituted body replacing one stolen from a cross and thereby saving the soldier from punishment. The third and last is a brief statement concerning the notoriety of the event and the reaction of people to it.

When reduced to this bare and generalized outline, the Latin versions are remarkably reminiscent of a similar outline of the Christian gospels and the Acts of the Apostles. There, too, are the same three divisions: a virgin who gives birth to a child and becomes an object of suspicion; a crucified body offered for others; and a sequel describing results of the account. Could the Phaedrian-Petronian story be a parody of the Christian theme? The dates of the Latin writers coincide with the days of Christ's ministry and the early years of the church. Petronius had spent some time in eastern Mediterranean lands. And the usual contemptuous pagan attitude toward Christianity would have encouraged them to poke fun at the new religion. It is therefore entirely within the realm of possibility that the Latin story bears some relationship to Christian preaching, thought, and incipient literature.

There remains the question of probability. Hardly had the Christian mission been inaugurated when there arose in many minds doubts and on many lips sneers and jibes about the virgin birth. Some of them are embedded in the Gospel texts and even more in apocryphal legends.[2] The crucifixion of Christ and the doctrine of the atonement are the most prominent features of Christianity and both would and did attract far more attention than the dogma of the virgin birth. The pages of the New Testament ring with this complex of doctrines and would certainly provoke heathen comment. The well-known Palatine *graffito* (the crucified creature with horse's head and the inscription, "Alexamenos worships his god"), whatever its exact date, is evidence that the comic muse was early at work on this central aspect of the Christian religion. That there should be a sequel, some kind of statement of reaction, requires no special attention.

In the course of the second century there were published in Greek two notable satires on the Christian story, namely, the *Death of Peregrinus* by Lucian of Samosata (*ca.* 170) and the *True Discourse* by Celsus (*ca.* 178).[3] The former is not so striking in detail, but the satire is obvious. Peregrinus is definitely compared with Christ (section 11) and is at length immolated dramatically (section 36). Lucian wrote another book, a dialogue called *The Runaways*, which recounts the consequences of the death of Peregrinus.[4] In these two writings we have, as it were, a Gospel and Acts of Peregrinus.

The work by Celsus is far more significant and circumstantial. Here is an outstanding attack in great detail. Jesus is portrayed as the offspring of an adulterous union of a poor Jewish country woman (I, xxviii) and a soldier named Panthera (I, xxxii). The reality of His death and resurrection is lengthily challenged and the reaction to His life, death, and presumed resurrection is questioned (Book II). The entire refutation is moreover attributed to a Jew, whom Celsus has created as one of his chief protagonists.

The last point suggests that there was a Jewish version mocking or parodying the Gospel and Acts. This consideration lends credence to Hugh J. Schonfield's attempt to establish the antiquity of at least the nucleus of the *Toldoth Jeshu*.[5] In such a case, therefore, there was still another, a third, early parody, which in its original form or as an oral version may have antedated Lucian's stories and Celsus' attack or at the latest have been contemporaneous with them.

Since there were actual and known instances of parody of the Christian story, it is obvious that it is not only possible but indeed probable that there is some relationship between the "matron of Ephesus" tale and the Christian tradition. It has been twice elsewhere suggested that Petronius (and *ipso facto* Phaedrus) not only had some knowledge of Christian teaching, but did in fact make verbal use of it.[6] And it has already been intimated that the two Latin versions bear an overall resemblance to the Christian gospel and that they

are not related to folklore.[7] It is in consequence reasonable
to suppose that the "matron" story is the earliest known
parody of the Christian account, that it inaugurates in the
literary sphere the mocking tradition that was followed by
Lucian, Celsus, and the author of the *Toldoth Jeshu*, and
indeed even in the present day by William Faulkner in *A
Fable*.[8]

9

A Note

on the Date of the

Great Advent Antiphons

The Great Advent Antiphons, also called the Great O's, are among the most beautiful and impressive elements in the Christian liturgy. They are the proper anthems for Magnificat at Vespers from 17 December to 23 December. Contrary to the usual rule for ferial days, they are sung in full at the beginning as well as at the end of the canticle.

The dating of these liturgical gems has attracted some attention. The view most commonly held is that of Fernand Cabrol, O.S.B., who developed the theory that the liturgy of Advent was completed during the seventh to ninth centuries, with only slight additions, particularly the Great O's, being made thereafter.[1]

A different theory has been brought forward by Herbert Thurston, S.J., who has attempted to show that the Anglo-Saxon Cynewulf, in his poem *Christ* (*ca.* 800), was familiar with these antiphons.[2] He indeed considered the entire work:

a sort of glorification of the ecclesiastical season of Advent, and in particular the first division or canto of the poem is seen to be founded almost exclusively upon the text of the "Great O's," which are simply paraphrased one after another, and worked with considerable literary skill into the text of the poem.[3]

He therefore concluded: "Every indication seems to me to show that these antiphons are much older than the ninth century, and I know no valid reason for regarding them as posterior to the rest of the Roman Antiphonary or to the time of Pope Gregory the Great himself." [4]

Thurston had the edge of the argument, but Cabrol incorporated his view unchanged in his *Dictionnaire d'archéologie chrétienne et de liturgie*, although referring to Thurston's article in a footnote.[5]

In order to give further circumstantial evidence for dating these antiphons in the time of Pope Gregory the Great (590–604), Thurston pointed out that the initial letters (that is, after the "O") of the antiphons, the order reversed, spell the Latin sentence, *Ero cras*, which he translated, "I [Christ] will be (with you) tomorrow." Referring to the well-known fact that such early writers as Ennodius (473–521) and Fulgentius (480–550) delighted in this kind of childish triviality, he suggested that this might imply an equally early date for the antiphons.[6] This, of course, proves too much, for one can get as good an acrostic by including the most familiar imitation of the Great O's, *O Virgo virginum*. This would provide us with the words "*Vero cras*," which could presumably be translated, "Verily (I will be with you) tomorrow"!

There is, however, more direct evidence that leads me to think it is entirely within the realm of possibility and even of probability that the Great O's may be dated still earlier, before Gregory the Great, in fact about the time of Boethius (482–524). It is to that I now want to turn.

There is a passage in the *Consolation of Philosophy* that seems, consciously or unconsciously, to be a "tag" from the first of the Great Antiphons, *O Sapientia*. It reads: "Est igitur summum, inquit [Philosophia], bonum quod regit *cuncta fortiter suaviterque disponit*." [7] Compare with this the text of *O Sapientia:* "O Sapientia, quae ex ore Altissimi prodiisti, attingens a fine usque ad finem, *fortiter suaviterque disponens omnia:* Veni ad docendum nos viam prudentiae."[8] The antiphon is based on a passage of Scripture: "Attingit [Sapientia] ergo a fine usque ad finem *fortiter et disponit omnia suaviter*." [9]

The question logically arises, Was Boethius quoting from the liturgy or from the Biblical text? [10] The eminent scholar of the Mass Adrian Fortescue considers this the most certain *(certissima)* quotation of Scripture in the entire *Consolatio*.[11] W. Weinburger also annotates this place in his edition with a reference to the passage from the book of Wisdom, intimating however that E. K. Rand deemed it only a chance agreement with the Biblical text.[12]

It would be remarkable if this were the only exact citation from the Bible in a book so definitely influenced by Scriptural teaching and filled with so many opportunities for appropriate quotation.[13] I therefore believe that Boethius' words are a reminiscence of the Great Antiphon and only indirectly from the Bible by way of the antiphon. For instance, the order of the words, *fortiter suaviterque disponit* (antiphon: *disponens*), is precisely that of *O Sapientia*, not that of the Bible text. The quotation is presumably unconscious, being simply a rhythmical and haunting phrase re-

called by the imprisoned philosopher from his memory of
the liturgy.

Thurston has proved that knowledge of these antiphons
antedates the ninth century and has cited traditional indications that they belong to the age of Gregory the Great. It
seems to me that the Boethian passage establishes one, *O Sapientia*, and by implication probably the other six, as known
and used as early as the beginning of the sixth century.

10

Beowulf and the Liturgy

To approach *Beowulf* from the standpoint of antique Christian tradition is to be unavoidably impressed with its Christian coloration—and this despite the nonappearance of specific doctrinal references.[1] Although the story itself is certainly a composite of heathen tales of the early Northland, yet as a finished product by the hand of a courtly and Christian Anglo-Saxon poet in the era of Bede it falls within a "golden age" of Old English learning derived from both Graeco-Roman and ecclesiastical sources. More particularly as one reads the middle section, an account of the struggle with Grendel's mother, he observes a rather strange suggestion of Patristic theological speculation about Christ's "harrowing of hell."[2] Indeed this is adumbrated by Klaeber in his remark that "we need not hesitate to recognize features of the Christian Savior in the destroyer of hellish fiends, the warrior gentle and brave, blameless in thought and deed, the king that dies for his people. Nor is the possibility of discovering direct allusions to the person of the Savior to be ignored."[3]

We may notice the following points in the section about Grendel's mother. First, the mere in which Grendel and his mother lived and into which Beowulf plunged is identified by the poet as hell (lines 852, 1274), an identification that is perhaps strengthened by the statements that it is a water weirdly aflame (1365f.), reminiscent of the Apocalyptic "lake which burneth with fire and brimstone: which is the second death" (Revelation 21:8; 19:20, etc.; cf. Old Latin versions of Matthew 3:15); and that it is a habitation of sea-monsters and sea-worms (1425–1430, 1510–1512; cf. Mark 9:44, 46, 48; Isaiah 66:24). Secondly, Beowulf prepares for his descent as though for death. As he girds himself, the hero mourns not at all for life (1442); as he addresses Hrothgar, he gives directions in the event of his dying (1477f.). The parallel with Christ is even more striking as Beowulf magnanimously forgives his enemy Unferth just before the plunge into the fen-depths (1488–1490; cf. Luke 23:34). Third, the descent itself is depicted as a victorious military campaign against the powers below (1441–1471; cf. Colossians 2:15; I Corinthians 2:8; Revelation 1:18; 19:15; Psalm 24:7–10). Fourth, at the moment of victory a beam of preternatural light penetrates the dismal scene beneath the waters and brightens it (1570–1572; cf. Isaiah 4:2; Luke 1:78f.).[4] Fifth, in the meanwhile back on the edge of the mere, all the onlookers, except Beowulf's own faithful Geats, supposing that the hero has been killed, give up the vigil at the ninth hour of the day (1594–1602).[5] It will be recalled immediately and inevitably that it was at the very same hour that Christ, abandoned by all but the most faithful few, died on the cross (Matthew 27:46; Mark 15:34, 37; Luke 23:44–46). Sixth, the returning champion brings with him trophies of his victory (1612–1615; cf. Colossians 2:15). Finally, there is a suggestion of winter's end and springtime's burgeoning as Beowulf comes up in triumph (1608–1611), which, although not strictly Biblical, is one of the most ancient of Easter themes.

Thus, in succession of ideas and motifs, there is a significant parallel between Beowulf's adventure and Christ's death, harrowing of hell, and resurrection. Closer examination, however, reveals that apparent similarities to the "harrowing" are enveloped, as within widening concentric circles, by allusions to the deluge and creation. For instance, the sword hilt, one of the trophies brought up from the struggle by Beowulf, was the work of giants who lived before the flood. On it were runes telling of their ancient battles (1677–1698), presumably against God (113f.; cf. Genesis 4:22; 6:3f., 17). The mention of Cain's fratricide, outlawry, exile, and begetting of ancestors of Grendel 1261–1267) recalls the more elaborate treatment earlier in the poem where one of the scops in Heorot sings a song of creation, of beauty-bright land wrought by the Almighty in the midst of encompassing waters, of sun and moon set as light to land-dwellers, of leafy woods adorning regions of earth, and of human life shaped by the same Eternal (90–114).[6] It was this song uttered to music of the harp that incited Grendel, of the evil brood of Cain, to his depredations (99–114).

We have therefore, in the account of Beowulf's encounter with Grendel's mother, a strong central reminiscence of Christ's harrowing of hell that widens to include recollections, next, of the deluge, and then of creation. We may now inquire where else we have the same complex of ideas. The answer is to be found in rites associated with Christian baptism. In the ancient church these were exceedingly prolonged, occupying the entire period of Lent and culminating in the actual ceremony on Holy Saturday.[7] By the sixth and seventh centuries, however, they had been somewhat curtailed; and, although they were no longer reserved for Lenten and Paschal seasons, and although the catechumenate had fallen into virtual desuetude, the traditional teaching concerning baptism was preserved in the liturgy of Holy Saturday.

Originally a candidate for baptism was examined at the beginning of Lent about his character, disposition, and intention by the bishop, who then enrolled his name in the register. The allegoresis of ancient theologians interpreted the questioning as recalling the temptation (trying, testing) of Christ, thus a conflict with Satan, hence similar to the temptation of Adam; and the registering of the name as an anticipation of recording of the name in the book of life. Lent itself was one long preparation for baptism with frequent exorcisms of the candidate because Satan (serpent, dragon) was barring at every turn the road to salvation.[8]

The grand climax came on Holy Saturday. The ceremonies began with blessing of the new fire, readying and lighting of the Paschal candle accompanied by the singing of *Exultet*, solemn reading of the twelve "prophecies," and blessing of the font. Then came the administration of baptism. In the baptistery (usually an octagonal structure), often embellished with portrayal of the Good Shepherd and His sheep amid beautiful trees and flowers, a fountain nearby where harts slaked their thirst, directly opposite a representation of the fall and expulsion of Adam and Eve from Paradise, the candidate, facing westward, renounced the devil and all his pomps; then, facing eastward, he professed allegiance to Christ. Anointed with holy oil, like an athlete made ready for a struggle, and signed with the proprietary and protective *sphragis* (seal) of the cross, thus rendered redoubtable against demons, the neophyte entered the bap-

tismal pool. Saint Cyril of Jerusalem referred to this particular act as a descent into the waters of death, into the habi-
tat of the sea-dragon, just as Christ went down into Jordan
where dwelled the monster Behemoth (Job 40:15, 23). The
font is therefore both burial place of the old Adam and
maternal womb of the new Adam. After baptism there
followed the litany and first Mass of Easter.

It is of special importance to scrutinize more closely the
content of *Exultet* and the twelve prophecies, for they are
the proximate source of Patristic teachings about the symbolism of baptism. Sung in the grave tone of the Gospel,
Exultet blesses Christ, who paid for us the debt of Adam's
transgression; commemorates the passage of Israel dry-shod
through the Red Sea led by a pillar of fire; adverts to the
triumphant harrowing of hell; and exults over the moment
of resurrection by which "night shall shine as day." When
the officiant has inserted into the Paschal candle grains of
incense, the chant is resumed, begging God to accept this
"work of the bees." The same thought follows the lighting
of the candle, which is "nourished by the melting wax which
the bee as a mother has brought forth for the sustenance of
this precious light." Thereupon ensued a curious Vergilian
digression (later deleted by the church) which is here presented in full.[9]

The bee excels other living creatures which have been
made subject to man. Although it is least in bodily size, it
cherishes great thoughts within its small breast; it is weak in
strength but strong in talent. When the round of seasons
has been completed, when frosty winters have laid aside
their hoariness and springtime's mildness has supplanted icy
decay, immediately to it comes zeal for advancing to labor.
Scattered through the fields, wings poised delicately, legs
uncertain, they settle suddenly with mouth to suck the blos-
soms. Laden with their nourishment, they wander back to

the hive. And there with incredible art they build little cells with firm glue; some compress the flowing honey, some turn flowers into wax, others form offspring with the mouth, still others envelope the nectar with leaves gathered together. O truly blessed and marvelous bee! The males never violate the other sex, they do not shatter the embryo, nor do births destroy chastity! Thus the holy Virgin Mary conceived: as a Virgin she brought forth and as a Virgin she remained.

After the conclusion of *Exultet*, there begins the reading of a series of twelve lessons, each "explained" by a brief collect. The first reading (Genesis 1:1–31; 2:1–2) sets forth the majestic story of creation; the second (Genesis 5, 6, 7, 8), the account of the deluge, the saving of Noah's family in the ark, and the new covenant; the third (Genesis 22:1–19), the sacrifice of Isaac; the fourth (Exodus 14:24–31; 15:1), the crossing of the Red Sea and destruction of Pharaoh's host (this is followed by singing of the canticle of Moses, Exodus 15:1, 2); the fifth (Isaiah 54:17; 55:1–11), a veiled oracular promise of baptism and Eucharist; the sixth (Baruch 3:9–38), a contrast between deceitful wisdom of the world and the supernatural character of Divine wisdom; the seventh (Ezekiel 37:1–14), the vision of the valley of dry bones; the eighth (Isaiah 4:1–6), a vision of the ultimate purification and glory of Zion (followed by the canticle of the vineyard, Isaiah 5:1, 2, 7); the ninth (Exodus 12:1–11), an account of the institution of Passover; the tenth (Jonah 3:1–10), Jonah's preaching to Nineveh and the repentance of that city; the eleventh (Deuteronomy 31:22–30), Moses' exhortation to fidelity (followed by the canticle of Deuteronomy 32:1–4), and the twelfth (Daniel 3:1–24), the story of the Three Children in the fiery furnace.

It is worthy of note that the succession of theological allusions in *Beowulf* (creation, deluge, harrowing of hell, resurrection) finds interesting parallels in *Exultet* (where the catalogue is Adam's guilt, passage of the Red Sea, harrowing of hell, resurrection) and in the prophecies (where the catalogue is creation, deluge, sacrifice of Isaac, passage of the Red Sea, a vague prophecy, a Wisdom reference, the valley of dry bones, another prophecy, the Paschal institution, Jonah's preaching, an exhortation, and the fiery furnace). All of the allusions, Biblical and Beowulfian, were used by the Church Fathers as types or symbols of Christian baptism. It seems therefore that the middle section of *Beowulf* is quite heavily laden with a complex of ideas that presuppose familiarity with the baptismal liturgy. It is of added significance that the ancient *Exultet* that the author of *Beowulf* may have known contained that strange and irrelevant eulogy of the bee, indeed it is suggestive if the name Beowulf is correctly interpreted as "Bee-wolf" or "Bee-foe" (that is, "Bear").[10]

However heathen the original story was, it is surely reasonable to suppose that the account of Beowulf's descent into the grim fen, his encounter with the demon-brood staining the water with blood, and his triumphant emergence from it into joyous springtime is, at the least, a reflection of the liturgy of baptism; at the most, an allegory of it.[11] That this view is not on a priori grounds impossible is evident from the quite elaborate Christian allegories of Cynewulf and of the Caedmonian *Exodus*, both approximately contemporary with the *Beowulf*-poet. Indeed the *Exodus* shows precisely the influence of the same twelve Holy Saturday prophecies.[12] And, interestingly enough, it reflects a knowledge of just that portion of *Beowulf* with which we are here concerned.[13] Since it has been demonstrated that the

Exodus shows the effect of the ancient liturgy of baptism and Holy Saturday, one goes not too far afield in presuming that a similar relationship exists in reference to *Beowulf*.

If we can place the compilation of *Beowulf* within the generous period between 650 and 825, it is worth recalling that the rite of baptism was of peculiar importance. First, during the seventh century it was being very frequently performed in England, often under impressive circumstances and often upon massed numbers of converts.[14] Second, during the eighth century there was a like situation among the Continental kinsmen of the Anglo-Saxons.[15] Third, near the end of the eighth century and beginning of the ninth, it even became an instrument of policy in the political, military, and diplomatic exploits of Charlemagne. Moreover, the Frankish ruler evoked from many of his prelates detailed discussions of the ceremonies of the rite.[16] We may therefore add *Beowulf* to the *Exodus* and the *Christ* as evidence of debt to the liturgy, for, as Bright has said, "doctrine and rite had control of the popular consciousness and were . . . available for artistic treatment." [17] Lawrence has made an equally significant observation that is pertinent: "the audience obviously waited with no less eagerness for reminiscences of old historic tradition. Almost every page of *Beowulf* gives evidence of how completely this filled their minds. The poet had only to suggest, in order to evoke vivid recollections." [18] This remark could apply just as well for the liturgical element in the Christian tradition, which is surely evoked in the account of Beowulf's encounter with Grendel's mother.

11

Joseph of Arimathea
and a Chalice

In 1920 Miss Jessie L. Weston asserted that "there is no Christian legend concerning Joseph of Arimathea and the Grail." She continued: "Neither in Legendary, nor in Art, is there any trace of the story; it has no existence outside the Grail literature, it is the creation of romance, and no genuine tradition." [1] The foregoing words echo Miss Weston's earlier view expressed in 1913, in which she had pointed out "the absolute dearth of ecclesiastical tradition with regard to the story of Joseph and the Grail." [2] Only seven years later, in 1927, William A. Nitze, in his edition of Robert de Boron's *Le roman de l'estoire dou Graal*, commented on the "book" referred to in lines 932ff. of the poem that it was "doubtless some edifying treatise like the *Gemma animae* by Honorius Augustodunensis." [3]

The passage that Nitze cited may be translated as follows:

While the priest is saying, "Per omnia saecula saeculorum," [4] the deacon comes, lifts up the chalice before him, covers part of it with the corporal, representing Joseph of

Arimathea who took Christ's body down, covered His face with a napkin, placed it in a tomb, covered it with a stone. Here the sacrifice [*oblata*] and the chalice are covered with the corporal, which signifies the clean shroud in which Joseph wrapped the body of Christ. The chalice signifies the sepulcher; the paten, the stone which closed the sepulcher....[5]

Still later Pierre le Gentil also mentioned Honorius[6] and so did Miss Helen Adolf.[7] The latter in her notes made an additional reference to Hildebert of Tours.[8] Research since Miss Weston's book has therefore refuted her emphatic and positive words quoted above. There is a "trace of the story" of Joseph and a chalice apart from Grail literature; it is not "the creation of romance." It remains now to demonstrate that there was a "genuine tradition" associating Joseph of Arimathea with a chalice, not indeed as early as Glastonbury fans might desire, nor even geographically close to Glastonbury, but early enough and close enough.

Those writers who have referred to Honorius might have inquired into his sources, for we may assume that he was not original. In fact some of his contemporaries made assertions quite similar to his. Rupert of Deutz, for example, has the following:

> Then the deacon approaches and for a moment lifts the sacrifice reverently from the altar; then just like the priest himself puts it down again, because Joseph of Arimathea and Nicodemus, too, came with the centurion and, begging the body of Jesus from Pilate, took it down and buried it. They buried it, I say, a fact signified to us when the chalice is again covered with the corporal.[9]

Obviously we are entitled to ask the origin of this exegesis. Fortunately the answer does not lie far afield. The fountainhead of all such allegorical interpretation of the Liturgy was Amalarius of Metz (died *ca.* 850).[10] Here I take the liberty of citing a lengthy passage from his very influential work:

> While they were thus looking on, there came "a man named Joseph who was a councillor, a good and upright man. He had not agreed to their plan or deeds. From Arimathea, a city of Judea, he too was looking for the kingdom of God. This one approached Pilate and requested the body of Jesus. When it was taken down he wrapped it in a shroud and placed it in a rock-hewn tomb in which no one had yet been placed." [11]

Although he had been one of the secret disciples, he publicly surpassed them all, both disciples and apostles. For while the disciples were only standing a long way off and looking on, while the apostles were even hiding away in secret places, Joseph purchased the shroud to wrap the dead body of Jesus. Of what great importance this Joseph was is mentioned in Bede's commentary on Luke: "Joseph was indeed of high dignity in the eyes of the world, but he is honored as having been of greater favor in the eyes of God. For through the uprightness of his merits he was deemed worthy to bury the Lord's body and through the eminence of his political power he was able to secure possession of it. An unknown person could not have gone to a presiding official and demanded the body of a crucified man." [12]

The archdeacon who lifts the chalice along with the priest holds eminence among other deacons, so also this Joseph who was counted worthy to take the Lord's body down from the cross and bury it in his own tomb held eminence among the other disciples. Formerly the same man was reckoned to stand with the apostles, since he had once hidden for fear of the Jews.

The priest who elevates the sacrifice [*oblata*] represents Nicodemus, of whom John relates: "Moreover Nicodemus, who had first come to Jesus by night, also came bringing a mixture of myrrh and aloes, about a hundred pounds. They therefore took the body of Jesus and wrapped it in linen cloths with spices, as it is the custom of the Jews to bury." [13] With the sacrifice the priest makes two crosses near the chalice, to teach that He who was crucified for the

two people has been taken down from the cross. The elevation by both priest and deacon signifies Christ's deposition
from the cross.

A napkin is known to have been over the head of Jesus,
for John observes that Peter saw "the linens placed and the
napkin which had been over the head" of Jesus.[14] The sacrifice and chalice signify the Lord's body. When Christ said,
"This is the chalice of my blood," [15] He signifies His own
blood. As the wine is inside the chalice, so was this blood
inside the body.[16]

We may safely state that all later liturgiologists were employing not only the method but also the material of Amalarius whether they acknowledged indebtedness or not. And
well they might have hesitated to mention his name, for his
writings had, in part at least, been condemned as heretical.
We must now, however, go a step further and ask the source
from which Amalarius derived his theories.

Although it is known to us that Amalarius had two prede-
cessors who treated the Liturgy allegorically, one a Latin
writer, the other a Greek, he was apparently not aware of
them.[17] The practice of treating Scripture and theology as
allegory is, of course, very old, reaching back into the Bible
itself, receiving a tremendous impetus at the hands of Origen,
and having a continuous history throughout the Middle
Ages. This method Amalarius probably learned from the
Venerable Bede by way of Alcuin.[18] But his application of
it to the Liturgy was certainly his own. Indeed he claimed
the immediate inspiration of God for his interpretation, particularly in reference to the Joseph-chalice complex. In what
was perhaps the latest revision of his great masterpiece, he
wrote:

Quite recently it was revealed to me (I believe by the one
who opens and no one closes) what could be reasonably
said about the Lord's body placed on the altar and about

the chalice beside it, without violating the teaching of those who seek to explain to me in other and better ways how and why the bread is differently placed on the altar and the chalice near it.

From that place in the Canon where it is written, "Unde et memores sumus," [19] the altar is Christ's cross, down to the point at which the chalice is wrapped in the napkin of the deacon, in the place of Joseph who wrapped the Lord's body in a shroud and napkin. . . .[20]

It may eventually be possible to go further back than Amalarius, but not at the present stage of investigation. Amalarius was the first writer, so far as we now know, to present Joseph of Arimathea with a chalice in his hand. And it was from him that authors like Honorius of Autun and Rupert of Deutz learned, as (according to Nitze and others) it was from them that Robert de Boron adapted. From Amalarius of Metz, who died more than three hundred years before Robert, there is a direct line through the liturgical scholars of the Middle Ages to Honorius and even later ones.[21] If Nitze's note alluding to Honorius is correct—and it is obviously accepted by other scholars—a "genuine tradition" that is not "the creation of romance" did exist; a "Christian legend" concerning Joseph of Arimathea and a chalice did exist "outside the Grail literature." If, moreover, Amalarius' claim to originality and direct inspiration is true —and there is at present no documentary evidence to contradict it—the rapprochement of Joseph and the chalice is a result of the intuitive and creative imagination of Amalarius himself, a feat of which, in view of its consequences, he could well be inordinately proud.[22]

12

Alleluia:

A Word and Its Effect

"The iron of the heathen gleamed" [1] and the monastery of Jumièges went up in flames. As the brethren fled from the Northmen with whatever they could carry in their hands, one brother, a priest, put in his knapsack an antiphonary. Sometime later, still in the second half of the ninth century, the weary priest trudged up to the gate of the monastery of Saint Gall where he sought and received hospitality. And so after one brief, fleeting moment, the nameless brother disappeared from history, but not before he had left an indelible mark on Western literature. For it chanced that at Saint Gall there was a young brother named Notker, called "the Stammerer" *(Balbulus)*, born about 840, who demonstrated interest in the antiphonary rescued by the monk of Jumièges.

Notker tells us that he had great difficulty trying to memorize the long ornate melodies in the Alleluia chant of the church's liturgical music, for the improvements in musical notation ascribed to Guido of Arezzo yet lay more than a century and a half in the future. Modestly attributing failure to his "fickle memory," Notker had, therefore, while still quite young, attempted quietly and privately to devise a scheme by which he could retain the notes in his mind. But he was unsuccessful. It was then that he happened to examine the new brother's antiphonary. He observed that some additional words had been clumsily interpolated at the end of the Alleluia (apparently to assist in memorizing the melody). He was delighted at the convenient method, but disappointed at its rudimentary quality.

Immediately Notker set about to imitate and improve what he had learned. The result was two sequences that he submitted to his teacher, Iso, for criticism. The latter was pleased with his student's zeal and sympathetic with his lack of skill. In order to help in polishing the work, he made a valuable suggestion. "Every note of the song," he said, "should have its separate syllable." With this important criticism Notker returned to his project for further development.

He discovered that he could easily improve the words inserted at the last syllable of Alleluia. Interpolations at the second and third syllables, however, were so difficult that at first he deemed them impossible, although he later succeeded. The process must have been an extended one of trial and error, for by the time he presented his next sequences to an instructor, it was no longer Iso but Marcellus who was supervising his study. Marcellus was so impressed that he caused them to be officially transcribed and to be sung by the several choirs of the monastic school.[2]

The particular form thus contrived is called a *sequence* from the fact that, *following* the Alleluia before the Gospel at Mass, it is a prolongation of the final syllable. Initially it was, as we have seen, a mnemonic device to help singers remember the elaborate melody of that first syllable. At the beginning also it was simply rhythmical prose. Also there was a primary tendency to end each major word (or musical phrase) with the letter -*a*. In time, however, its lines became measured poetry rhyming in -*a*. Later other rhymes were introduced, not only in other letters, but also in more than one syllable. In a still further development, the compositions became dissociated from the Alleluia melody and the poems became independent compositions, reaching a peak in the glorious sequences of the school of Saint Victor. Moreover the sequence had hardly been born when it gave rise to its secular counterpart. It is worth noting that the attachment of sequence to Alleluia is still attested by the trochaic rhythm of both.[3,4]

Etymologically, Alleluia is composed of two Hebrew words meaning "praise ye" *(hal 'lu)* "the Lord" *(Jah)*. It is employed frequently in the book of Psalms,[5] where it is a liturgical chant of jubilation or a joyful response to such a chant used on festival occasions. It would appear that even so early the word was more an expression of vigorous, though formal, exultation than a devout literal statement. Elsewhere in the Old Testament it occurs only in Tobit 13:18, "All her [Jerusalem's] lanes will cry, 'Alleluia!' and will give praise, saying, 'Blessed is God who has exalted you for ever.' "[6] Another quasi-Biblical reference is III Maccabees 7:13, "Then they applauded his [Ptolemy Philopator's] words, as was proper, their priests and all the people; and they departed with joy, shouting the Alleluia."[7] It is obvious here, too, that, although the word might retain its etymological significance, it had been detached from Psalmody and had possibly embarked on an independent existence in which it was an ecstatic, joyous cry, perhaps spontaneous rather than liturgical. In this respect it is noteworthy that the early Greek and Latin versions generally retained the Hebrew expression by transliteration rather than translation, thus preserving the ambivalence.

Despite the importance of Alleluia in pre-Christian Judaism, its use in Christian circles is strangely attested no earlier than the book of Revelation (Apocalypse).[8] This book was the channel by which the word entered Christian usage, or rather it is presumably evidence that the word was employed in the primitive Christian liturgy. In the Revelation the word is used as it was in Judaism: as a part of (or antiphon on) Psalmody or hymnody and as a detached exclamation. About a century or more later Tertullian witnessed to much the same practice.[9]

So Alleluia began its journey through the centuries under Christian auspices to carry on the glorious tradition of Judaism along with the older religion. To both faiths it was equally a song of angels and men. Both tended to elaborate musically the last syllable until it became a pure, wordless chant of joy, perhaps related to the curious phenomenon called "speaking with tongues" (or technically, "glossolalia").[10] In both religions there were occasions on which the word virtually disappeared, became disembodied, spiritualized, and only the vowels were sung.[11] On the other hand, there appeared an opposing tendency to multiply the word, as in the case of the hundred and twenty-three Alleluias in the chanting of Hallel (Psalms 113–118, Revised Standard Version). In any case it had entered the Western tradition, where it had its greatest development.

In the West the employment of Alleluia has been manifold. Not only did it enter the liturgy (both Eucharist and Divine Office), but also popular usage. Near the middle of the fifth century Saint Germanus of Auxerre entered the island of Britain to combat the Pelagian heresy. Having been a soldier before he was a priest, he promptly joined the Britons in their struggle against the Saxons and Picts. Outnumbered he led his troops into a location to prepare an ambush for the enemy. Ordering the priests and others to shout as and when he shouted, at an appropriate moment he raised the cry, "Alleluia!" The resounding noise of the ancient Hebrew word reverberating from the surrounding hills so frightened the foes that they fled.[12] In the second half of the same century the aristocratic bishop of Clermont, Sidonius Apollinaris, tells us about the hurly-burly of traffic on the Rhone and on the highways paralleling it: creaking carriages, weary travelers on foot, and straining longshoremen. Amid all the noise of busy commercial life could be heard the voices of the bargemen rhythmically shouting, "Alleluia!" and the river banks echoing the same refrain.[13]

About a half-century or more later the man who would become Pope Gregory I the Great was so fascinated by the information reaching him from the British Isles that he wrote: "Lo, the tongue of Britain which had known how to do nothing but utter barbarous gutturals has already begun to sing the Hebrew Alleluia in divine praises." [14] His famous pun, perhaps the best known in Western literature, is seldom cited beyond the first part ("Not Angles, but angels"). As a matter of fact there were two further parts of it, the third being his query about the Angle king. When Gregory was told that he was Aella, he immediately punned on the name, "Alleluia, the praise of God the Creator must be sung in those lands." [15] Quite properly, therefore, Saint Augustine, his missionary, entered Kent chanting a litany having an antiphon with the Alleluia.[16]

By the ninth century, its place fixed in the liturgy and its joyful expression on many tongues, Alleluia was the subject of exegesis and exposition. The great liturgical scholar, Amalarius, explained that Alleluia before the Gospel at Mass affected inwardly everyone who sang it, causing him to meditate how he ought to praise God and how he ought to rejoice in Him. The final note of wordless jubilation reminded one of that ultimate condition when the speaking of words would not be necessary, when the mind by meditation alone would be able to communicate its faith.[17] Alleluia was also a foretaste of the elect's eternal gladness as well as a praise of God. In singing it, therefore, the music should not be somber but exultant, anticipating the joy of the life to come, Alleluia being the harvest of all our worship.[18] Amalarius accepted and transmitted the tradition that Alleluia was celestial in origin, a song of angelic beings. He believed that, regardless of the great beauty and sweetness of the Tract (substituted for Alleluia in Lent), Alleluia was far more beautiful, being of a richer and nobler language, namely, Hebrew.[19]

Amalarius is also witness to the suppression of Alleluia in the liturgy during the period from Septuagesima to Easter.[20] This particular practice gave rise in a somewhat later time to a formal "farewell to Alleluia" in some of the Western liturgies, usually at Vespers on Saturday before Septuagesima. The tendency was to multiply repetition of Alleluia on that occasion, after which it would not be used again until the first Mass of Easter. For that service the hymn, "Alleluia dulce carmen," was written, probably in the eleventh century. Two stanzas (in modern translation from a recently published breviary) illustrate the practice:

> Alleluia cannot always
> Be our song while here below;
> Alleluia our transgressions

> Make us for a while forego;
> For the solemn time is coming
> When our tears for sin must flow.
>
> Therefore in our hymns we pray Thee,
> Grant us, blessed Trinity,
> At the last to keep Thine Easter
> In our home beyond the sky,
> There to Thee forever singing
> Alleluia joyfully.[21]

This cessation of Alleluia gave rise to excesses, including a ceremonial "deposition of Alleluia" that in turn contributed to popular folkloristic customs.[22] Inevitably there also arose a corresponding "welcome to Alleluia" or "return of Alleluia." For instance, at a pontifical celebration of the first Mass of Easter the deacon chanted these words, "I announce to you a great joy which is Alleluia." No ceremonial, however, developed for the return comparable to that for the departure of Alleluia. And all of the excrescences were eliminated by the late sixteenth century.[23]

One of the strange uses of Alleluia occurred in the year 1233. In a time of great stress itinerant friars wandered through northern Italy crying incessantly, "Alleluia! Alleluia! Alleluia!" The masses followed them in a revivalistic orgy of penitence and preaching. Reputed miracles were performed to add to the excitement and numerous frauds were perpetrated, all recounted by that garrulous Minorite named Salimbene.[24] The year was called "the great Alleluia." From this point it is only a hop, skip, and jump to the fantastic phenomena of American frontier religion in the eighteenth and nineteenth centuries, and from there to the profane use of the word in the hobo song, "Hallelujah, I'm a bum! Hallelujah, bum again!"

In the present day Alleluia survives in all its splendor in

the liturgy (for example, the glorious Alleluia of Mozart's Twelfth Mass) and in such sacred music as the Hallelujah Chorus of Handel's oratorio, "The Messiah." It lives also in its detached usage as ejaculatory prayers and shouts in Pentecostal services. It also continues to appear occasionally in purely secular situations. Down the centuries it has been not only an act of worship, but also a magic formula, a war cry, a signal, a joyous exclamation, a song of plowmen and boatmen, and perhaps a nursery song.[25] One scholar has deemed it the germinal cell of all hymn-singing.[26] And the great Cardinal J. B. F. Pitra has well said that the story of Alleluia is itself a poem.[27] The foregoing is only a fragment of that poem.

13

Shakespeare
and the Holy Rosary

To a person interested in study of the Christian liturgy, its history, practice, influence, and derivatives, perception of a liturgical allusion is sometimes the reward of conscious search, as, for example, in considering the Apocalypse or Pliny the Younger's celebrated letter to Emperor Trajan. More frequently it has been an accidental result of reading with another purpose in mind, as, for instance, while perusing the *Satiricon* of Petronius or *De consolatione philosophiae* of Boethius or the Anglo-Saxon epic, *Beowulf*.[1] In much the same manner there has arisen a suspicion that in the Shakespearean sonnets a subtle reflection of the liturgy may be discerned. To an investigation of that supposition I now turn.

Once the possibility of an association between Shakespeare's sonnets and a part of the liturgy or a derivative of it arises, an initial inspection reveals a certain resemblance between the structure of the poems and the Holy Rosary. From mid-sixteenth century onward the Rosary has consisted of one hundred and fifty-three Hail Marys divided into fifteen groups of ten and one of three, each group now introduced by Our Father and concluded by Gloria Patri. It is quite impressive therefore to observe that there are one hundred and fifty-four sonnets in the Shakespearean sequence, the last two being variants of the same theme. A second datum of some importance is the prominence of the word *rose* in the Sonnets.[2] That word is intimately related to the term *rosary* and is employed in at least one instance in medieval literature to mean the Rosary of Christian devotion.[3] These two rather obvious points, however, prove nothing; they merely emphasize the suspicion that requires still further inquiry.

Since the fifteenth century each decade of the Rosary has been devoted to a meditation on one of the fifteen "mysteries" in the life of Christ and the Blessed Virgin Mary. They are *The Joyful Mysteries*—(1) The Incarnation or annunciation of the Incarnation, (2) The Blessed Virgin's visit to her cousin Elizabeth, (3) The birth or nativity of Christ, (4) The purification of the Blessed Virgin, (5) Christ lost and found at the age of twelve or the finding of Christ in the Temple among the doctors; *The Sorrowful Mysteries*—(6) Christ's agony in Gethsemane, (7) His flagellation, (8) His being crowned with thorns, (9) His carrying the cross, (10) The crucifixion; *The Glorious Mysteries* —(11) The resurrection of Christ, (12) His ascension into heaven, (13) The coming of the Holy Ghost, (14) The assumption of the Blessed Virgin into heaven, and (15) Her coronation.

We may quickly test our theory about the sonnets by selecting fifteen poems at intervals of ten to determine whether they bear any resemblance to the fifteen mysteries. In order not to be too arbitrary I chose as starting point Sonnet VII.

(1) Of the first ten poems it conveys the strongest and clearest reminiscences of the Joyful Mystery of the Incarnation. As one reads lines 1–8, he inevitably recalls Psalm 18:6f. (Vulgate): "In sole posuit tabernaculum suum; et ipse tanquam sponsus procedens de thalamo suo. Exsultavit ut gigas ad currendam viam; a summo caelo egressio ejus. Et occursus ejus usque ad summum ejus; nec et qui se abscondat a calore ejus." [4] Parts of this passage occur as the antiphon on Magnificat at First Vespers of Christmas, as one of the antiphons in the first Nocturn of Matins of Christmas and Matins of the Octave of Christmas, and as the versicle and response at the end of that Nocturn on both Christmas and Christmas Octave. Under these circumstances the word *Orient* in line 1 of Sonnet VII recalls the Great Advent Antiphon, "O Oriens, splendor lucis aeternae et sol justitiae . . . ," proper to Magnificat on December 21. In view of the foregoing parallels we can quite justifiably state that verbally Sonnet VII may have some relation, however remote, to the first Joyful Mystery. It is therefore a convenient point of departure from which to begin a cursory inspection of the poems at intervals of ten.

(2) At first glance Sonnet XVII seems to reflect nothing of the second Joyful Mystery. Yet, strangely enough, the phrases, "in time to come" (line 1) and "The age to come" (line 7), make one think of the words, "ecce enim ex hoc beatam me dicent omnes generationes," [5] and "a progenie in progenies," [6] in the hymn of the Blessed Virgin. Still further, the references to poetry, "my verse" (line 1), "fresh numbers" (line 6), and "stretched miter of an Antique song" (line 12), remind us that the larger part of the Biblical narrative of the visitation is taken up with a typical Scriptural poem composed by the Blessed Virgin. Line 8, "Such heauenly touches nere toucht earthly faces," is certainly apt,

and so is line 13, "But were some childe of yours aliue that time."

(3) Sonnet XXVII contains some words which might be faint allusions to the Joyful Mystery of the Nativity. The references to "my bed" (line 1) and "trauaill tired" (line 2) are surely not inappropriate,[7] and "a zelous pilgrimage to thee" (line 6) might summon up remembrance of two pilgrimages to the newborn Messiah, that of the shepherds and that of the Magi. But, above all, lines 11f., "like a iewell (hunge in gastly night) / Makes black night beautious, recall a typical medieval conceit that the birth of Christ caused the night in which He was born to shine with preternatural light.[8]

(4) Lines 11f. of Sonnet XXXVII, "That I in thy abundance am suffic'd, / And by a part of all thy glory liue . . . ," an expression of intimate union of the poet and the person to whom the poem was addressed, suggest a phrase and an idea from the Gospel account of the fourth Joyful Mystery. The aged prophet Simeon, speaking to the Blessed Virgin, assures her that her indissoluble union with her Divine Son will mean that whatever happens to Him will happen also to her, "et tuam ipsius animam pertransibit gladius." [9] This thought and virtually these words reappear in the first stanza of the great medieval hymn, *Stabat Mater dolorosa.*

(5) The fifth Joyful Mystery is reflected throughout Sonnet XLVII by the suggestion of separation of the poet from the person to whom the poem was written, by the poet's longing for reunion, and by the anticipation of joy at reunion.

(6) Sonnet LVII is an excellent allusion to the first Sorrowful Mystery. Christ bade His disciples to wait and watch while He went farther to pray.[10] The entire sonnet is one about the waiting and watching of a slave who does the

master's bidding without understanding it. Especially impressive is line 5, "Nor dare I chide the world-without end houre," containing that phrase with which English liturgical prayers close ("world without end"), immediately evoking the thought of prayer. The word *houre* is also quite Scriptural in this context.[11]

(7) The flagellation (the second Sorrowful Mystery) is intimated by the phrases of Sonnet LXVII, "with his presence grace impietie" (line 2), "Why should he live, now nature banckrout is, / Beggerd of blood . . ." (lines 9f.), and "before these last [daies] so bad" (line 14).

(8) Lines 5–8 of Sonnet LXXVII may be vaguely suggestive of the suffering endured from the crowning with thorns (the third Sorrowful Mystery).

(9) On the other hand, Sonnet LXXXVII in its entirety is a beautiful expression of what one might feel in the presence of the fourth Sorrowful Mystery. The first line, "Farewell thou art too deare for my possessing," is eminently apt, but especially so are lines 5f., "For how do I hold thee but by thy granting, / And for that ritches where is my deserving?" as well as the phrase in line 9, "Thy selfe thou gau 'st."

(10) In a similar manner Sonnet XCVII is the sad reaction of one to the absence of his beloved, parallel to the grief of the disciples at the crucifixion (the fifth Sorrowful Mystery). Particularly apt are the words, "dark daies" (line 3), "old Decembers barenesse euery where" (line 4), and "thou away, the very birds are mute" (line 12).

(11) The parallels in Sonnet CVII to the first Glorious Mystery are unusually striking: the "eclipse indur'de" (line 5), the "sad Augurs" proven false in their "presage" (line 6), the end of "incertenties" (line 7), the peace and victory of "endlesse age" (line 8), and the assurance of "Ile liue" (line 11); perhaps also, "this most balmie time" (line 9) and

"My loue lookes fresh" (line 10). The phrase "tombes of brasse are spent" (line 14) immediately recalls the doctrine of the harrowing of hell and Christ's victorious assault on the gates of brass of the lower world.[12]

(12) The second Glorious Mystery is only vaguely intimated in Sonnet CXVII by lines 7f.: "That I haue hoysted saile to al the windes / Which should transport me farthest from your sight."

Up to this point the parallels between the Mysteries of the Holy Rosary and the Shakespearean Sonnets are impressive. But Sonnets CXXVII, CXXXVII, and CXLVII, which should on this theory agree in some manner with the third, fourth, and fifth of the Glorious Mysteries, do not, as a matter of fact, do so. Yet it is probably worthy of mention that, as the last two Mysteries shift from events in the life of Christ to events in the life of His mother, the earlier Sonnets (through CXXVI) seem to be directed to a man, while those after Sonnet CXXVI seem to be directed to a woman. Moreover, since three of the Hail Marys of the Rosary are used for meditation on the theological virtues of faith, hope, and charity (or love), it is rather curious to observe that Sonnet CLI has negative allusions to faith in the words, "gentle cheater" (line 3), "betraying" (line 5), and "treason" (line 6), while Sonnets CLIII and CLIV, variations on the same theme, are quite obvious allusions to (profane) love. Sonnet CLII should, of course, parallel in some way the virtue of hope, but instead alludes strongly to treachery, the opposite of faith.

Before proceeding further let us test the theory by selecting a few other sonnets at random to determine whether they may at intervals of ten suggest the Mysteries. We may do this briefly and schematically, beginning with Sonnet I (the enumeration in parentheses being that of the Mysteries

as listed earlier): (1) I, lines 1f., 4, 9f.; (2) XI, lines 1, 3f.;
(3) XXI, lines 6f., 11f.; (4) XXXI, no apparent resemblance; (5) XLI, lines 2, 10; (6) and (7) LI and LXI, no
apparent resemblances; (8) LXXI, lines 1f., 14; (9) LXXXI,
lines 1, 8; (10) XCI, lines 9–14; (11) CI, lines 11f.; (12)–
(15) CXI, CXXI, CXXXI, CXLI, no apparent resemblances.

Beginning with Sonnet III we have these results: (1) III,
lines 2, 5f., 9f.; (2) XIII, lines 1f., 7; (3) and (4), XXIII,
XXXIII, no apparent resemblances; (5) XLIII, lines 3, 9–
14; (6) LIII, line 5 (reference to Adonis); (7) LXIII, lines
3f.; (8) LXXIII, lines 2f., 5–8; (9) LXXXIII, lines 11f.;
(10) XCIII, lines 5, 9f., 13f.; (11) CIII, lines 5–12; (12)
CXIII, line 1; (13)–(15) CXXIII, CXXXIII, CXLIII, no
apparent resemblances.

And with Sonnet X, we have these results: (1) X, no apparent resemblance; (2) XX, the entire sonnet, especially
line 2; (3) XXX, lines 13f.; (4) XL, lines 1–4; (5) L, the
entire sonnet; (6) LX, the entire sonnet; (7) LXX, lines
2f.; (8) LXXX, no apparent resemblance; (9) XC, the entire sonnet; (10) C, no apparent resemblance; (11) CX, the
entire sonnet, especially lines 8f., 11–14; (12) CXX, no apparent resemblance; (13) CXXX, lines 1f. (reference to
red, the liturgical color for festivals of the Holy Ghost);
(14) and (15) CXL, CL, no apparent resemblances. It is
worth noting that in all four of our groups of sonnets there
are no seeming resemblances to the fourteenth and fifteenth
Mysteries.

Notwithstanding the fact that our scheme does not work
with absolute precision, we are entitled, I believe, to assume
that there is a similarity, however secular, of the sonnets to
the Holy Rosary. But we have yet to consider reasons for
the supposed resemblance. First, would William Shakespeare, nominally an Anglican, have made allusions to what

was in his day a peculiarly Roman Catholic practice? Of course the answer is "Yes." This point requires no belaboring, having been studied quite adequately by John Henry de Groot in his thesis, *The Shakespeares and "The Old Faith."* [13] I cite only one of many appropriate remarks from his volume:

> . . . there must have been occasions when out of the deep well of the subconscious there arose reminiscences of the Old Faith—thoughts and feelings of an almost nostalgic sort which, in becoming vivid to the artist, would take him back to the house on Henley Street. Once more he would hear the voice of his mother at prayer. In her he would see a faint reflection of Mary, the Virgin Mother of God. The very name would strengthen the association. Often, throughout the busy writing years, bits of Catholic imagery, Catholic sentiment, Catholic tradition, slipping unawares along the channels of the imagination, would enter the main stream of the poet's creative effort and give to that stream slight shifts of direction and touches of color discernible today in the poet's poems and plays. [14]

A second reason is even more relevant. It pertains to the sonnet tradition. Hardly had the sonnet been invented (in the thirteenth century) [15] when a development of it was contrived, namely, the sonnet-sequence. [16] Here we could go very far afield in quest of origins, but a few remarks must suffice. From its earliest days monasticism had encouraged, had indeed based its worship on, recitation of the Psalms in course. By early medieval times this practice was commuted for unlettered brothers to a comparable recitation of a hundred and fifty Paternosters, and by the time of the High Middle Ages was still further varied by substitution of Ave Marias for Psalms or Paternosters. The practice proved to be quite popular among the laity. Among literary persons there evolved by analogy a yet greater variation. Cycles of short poems or hymns in Latin, called *psalteria*, were composed, often original, but more often employing language of the corresponding Psalms or phrases from the Paternoster or, eventually, "tags" from the Ave Maria.[17] Similar works were composed in the European vernaculars. The influence of such poetry on sonnets and sonnet-sequences may not have been direct but it was unavoidable.[18]

Shakespeare's sonnets, however, are not religious. How, then, can they be associated with a religious background? To answer that question we introduce our third point. One of the commonest tendencies in medieval literature was toward parody,[19] whether in Latin or the vernaculars, in prose or verse, for serious purposes or profane use. One type of parody was artistic imitation of ecclesiastical texts: an example is the quaintly charming *Lay Folks Mass Book*.[20] Another type was the devotional multiplication of services parallel to the staple of Mass and Divine Office. The Rosary itself is an illustration of that. The third parodistic category includes neither the artistic, serious or profane, nor the votives, pious or superstitious, but secular imitations. This category may be further divided in a twofold manner: parodies that were serious, cynical, or satirical, written in an attempt to correct abuses; and those that had no object other than humor, mockery, or simple entertainment. An example is the late twelfth-century Anglo-Norman drinking song "Or hi parra," which imitates the eleventh-century hymn "Laetabundus." The extent to which parody was carried in the medieval period is almost inconceivable to us. Yet once we recognize that fact, we can understand how an utterly secular sequence might have had the Rosary as its ultimate background.

A fourth and final reason for suspecting that to be true of Shakespeare's sonnets is the immense importance of the

Rosary before and during the years in which he was beginning to write. The intricate history of the Rosary need not detain us, but a few facts must be recalled.[21] During the century before Shakespeare the Rosary devotion had been developed, spread, and popularized by such zealous enthusiasts as Dominic the Prussian, Alain de la Roche, and Henry Egher. The form was generally standardized, the Ave Maria was lengthened, and the usage of meditating on the Mysteries was added. Especially influential in promotion were organizations devoted to frequent use of the Rosary, notably one of Cologne established by the famous Dominican, James Sprenger, coauthor of *Malleus maleficarum*.[22] The Protestant Reformation served to accentuate its importance, since the Rosary was believed to be especially effective against heresy.[23]

When Shakespeare was only seven years of age, there occurred, on Sunday, October 7, 1571, that battle of Lepanto which Cervantes, Shakespeare's older contemporary, called "la mas memorable y alta ocasión que vieron los pasados siglos, ni esperan ver los venideros." [24] It was indeed a great victory, and popular opinion attributed it to processions that the Confraternity of the Holy Rosary had made that very day in Rome. The pope, Pius V, who only the year before had excommunicated (and deposed) Shakespeare's queen, immediately ordered a festival of the Rosary for the anniversary of the battle. In 1573 his successor, Gregory XIII, extended the commemoration as a major double to all churches in the Roman Catholic world having altars dedicated to the Rosary and increased the spiritual privileges attached to its use.[25] The fame of Lepanto must have been made even more vivid in England when, in 1576, the hero of the engagement, Don John of Austria, arrived in the Netherlands as the new governor. His presence just across the Channel was the occasion of many a plot to rescue the imprisoned Mary of Scotland and place her on the English throne with Don John as her consort.[26]

The year 1575, when Shakespeare was eleven years old, was a papal Holy Year or Jubilee. The persecuted English Roman Catholics could not, of course, participate in the celebration. But in order to allow them some part in the observance, Pope Gregory XIII made an exception in their case: a bull authorized a special arrangement whereby they might share the indulgences through prescribed recitations of the Rosary either in the form that has become customary or in the form called *Brigittine*.[27] Thus, whether Shakespeare ever used this devotion or not,[28] he must have been aware of its significance. And if our analysis of the sonnets is correct, they reflect it in a distant and thoroughly secular manner.

Epilogue

We have noted some instances of the pervasive influence of liturgy on our Western literatures through the sixteenth century. The beauty of the liturgy itself as literature has been intimated, but attention may be directed particularly to the collect. With its pure, chaste economy, and clarity, especially in its Latin form but also in the English of Archbishop Cranmer, it is a finely chiseled sentence that is still an object of admiration. The introit of Mass and responsory of the Divine Office—the former said or sung in the following manner: antiphon, Psalm, "Glory be," "As it was," antiphon repeated (A, B, C, D, A); and the latter in the following: response (two parts), response repeated, verse, second half of response, "Glory be," response repeated (AB, AB, C, B, D, AB)—aesthetically pleasing in their delicate repetitions, lent themselves to imitation in sensitive poetic forms, such as virelay, rondel, and ballade. A *chanson de geste* with its refrains seems moreover to bear some relation to the litany, and a lay to the sequence of

Mass. The sequence itself has already been mentioned above in connection with Alleluia.

The sixteenth-century divisions of Western Christianity did not destroy the impact; it became perhaps more tenuous, perhaps more subtle. As we have observed, the media of influence have been in verbal similarities or allusions, in certain forms, in a frame of reference for a story or poem, in providing an occasion for a literary product. These continued to be operative. Milton's ode *On the Morning of Christ's Nativity* and Bunyan's *Pilgrim's Progress*, however far removed from traditional liturgy, are witnesses to its perennial appeal. In seventeenth-century Russia the *Life of the Archpriest Avvakum by Himself* is almost wholly an account of liturgical disturbances that wracked the Russian church. (Svetlana Alliluyeva's name suggests that her maternal ancestors may have been involved.) Many of Robert Burns' poems reflect the meager liturgical practice of the Scottish church. Goethe and Walter Scott felt the influence, and both translated the *Dies irae*, sequence of Mass for the dead. (Berlioz and Liszt put the hymn to music.) Baudelaire, in his "infernal litanies," imitated church ritual, and in Anatole France's *Thais* there is a parody of *Victimae paschali*, the Easter sequence.

Liturgy provided a backdrop for T. S. Eliot's *Murder in the Cathedral* and Andrew Lytle's *At the Moon's Inn*, as well as for Joris-Karl Huysmans's *La Cathédrale, L'Oblat*, and *Là-Bas*. The delightful little poem that runs through Eugene O'Neill's lesser-known play, *The Fountain*, shows some affinity with the medieval *Ad perennis vitae fontem*. Even William Faulkner modeled *A Fable* on traditional accounts of Holy Week and in the death of his protagonist employed a motif derived from parody of an oral version of the Gospels.[1] And so it goes.

But a change is taking place. Since the middle of the twentieth century the Vulgate, with its sonorous Latin, and the Authorized Version, with its equally sonorous English, have been hurled from their thrones. Moreover, since the Second Vatican Council, the Latin Mass and its ancient Gregorian canon have fallen into desuetude and even the Edwardine Prayer Books have lost their prestige. Vast new efforts are under way to prepare fresh, contemporary, vernacular translations on an ecumenical basis.[2] But all this means that once more liturgy has been "rediscovered." Who knows or can guess what its impact will be in the future?

Notes

INTRODUCTION

1. Matt. 26:55; Mark 14:49; Luke 21:37; 24:53; John 2:13; Acts 2:46.

2. Acts 3:1; 5:20f., 42.

3. Eusebius, *Ecclesiastical History*, II, 23.

4. Ibid., V, 24.

5. Rom. 12:1; I Cor. 5:7; 10:1–4, 18; Phil. 4:18; Col. 2:11.

6. Heb. 8:5; 9:1–5, 23; cf. also Josephus, *Antiquities of the Jews*, III, 7, 7, and Philo, *Life of Moses*, III, 3–14. It is appropriate as a *general note* to mention J. Daniélou, *Bible et Liturgie* (Paris: Editions du Cerf, 1951); H. St. J. Thackeray, *The Septuagint and Jewish Worship*, 2nd ed. (London: Oxford University Press, 1923); T. H. Gaster, *Festivals of the Jewish Year* (New York: Sloane Associates, 1953); the brilliant paper by K. W. Clark, "Worship in the Jerusalem Temple after A.D. 70," *New Testament Studies*, 6 (July, 1960), pp. 269–80.

7. R. G. Moulton, *The Modern Reader's Bible* (New York: Macmillan, 1939); *The Psalms: A New Translation*, Grail ed. (Philadelphia: Westminster Press, 1963); *The Jerusalem Bible*, English ed. (Garden City, N. Y.: Doubleday and Co., 1966).

8. Ezek. 40–48.

9. Ezek. 43:10f.

10. Isa. 6:3; consult Eric Peterson, *The Angels and the Liturgy*, trans. R. Walls (New York: Herder and Herder, 1964).

11. Heb. 8:2, 5; 9:11, 23f.

12. Some important studies of the mysteries are F. Cumont, *Oriental Religions in Roman Paganism* (Chicago: Open Court, 1911); S. J. Case, *Experience with the Supernatural in Early Christianity* (New York: Century, 1929); H. R. Willoughby, *Pagan Regeneration* (Chicago: University of Chicago Press, 1929); S. Angus, *The Mystery-Religions and Christianity* (New York: Scribner's, 1925).

13. See descriptions in Angus, *Mystery-Religions*, pp. 123, 125.

14. Ignatius, *Romans*, vii, 3; *Smyrnaeans*, vii, 1; *Ephesians*, xiii, 1; xx, 2; *Philadelphians*, iv.

15. Justin Martyr, *(First) Apology*, lxvi.

16. Col. 1:15–21, 26; 2:8–23; 3:9–11, 23, and elsewhere.

17. Rom. 15:16.

18. The foregoing is a result of my forthcoming translation of the New Testament.

19. Walter Pater, *Marius the Epicurean* (London: Macmillan, 1924), p. 277; cited approvingly in E. J. Goodspeed, *The Meaning of Ephesians* (Chicago: University of Chicago Press, 1933), p. 60.

20. Cf., *inter alia*, Luke 1:46–55 *(Magnificat);* 1:68–79 *(Benedictus);* 2:29–32 *(Nunc dimittis).*

21. Matt. 6:9–13; Luke 11:2–4.

22. Most of the foregoing is summarized from my paper, "Liturgy-making Factors in Primitive Christianity," *Journal of Religion*, 23 (January, 1943), pp. 43–58, where fuller documentation is offered.

23. Philip Carrington, *The Primitive Christian Calendar*, vol. 1, Introduction and Text (Cambridge: University Press, 1952); and *According to Mark* (Cambridge: University Press, 1960).

24. Aileen Guilding, *The Fourth Gospel and Jewish Worship* (Oxford: Clarendon, 1960).

25. F. L. Cross, *I Peter: A Paschal Liturgy* (London: Mowbray, 1954).

26. This analysis, too, is a result of my forthcoming translation of the New Testament. See also my paper, "The Epistle of Saint James," *Journal of Bible and Religion*, 22 (January, 1954), pp. 27–29.

27. Non-Western evidence of its vitality and creativity may appear in two Coptic manuscripts in the library of the University of Mississippi. One, dated about the third century, is a papyrus codex of a hundred pages, single quire, containing Melito's *Peri Pascha*, II Macc. 6 ("the Jewish martyrs"), I Peter, Jonah, and an intriguing fragment of a hymn mentioning Joseph (of Arimathea?). Clearly it is a Paschal lectionary. The other, a parchment codex of the fifth century, sixty-six pages out of approximately one hundred and forty-six, contains Jer. 51:22–52:34 (LXX enumeration), Lamentations, Baruch 6, Baruch 1:1–2:2a, and Baruch 4:23–5:5, obviously a more developed Paschal lectionary. See Allen Cabaniss, "The University of Mississippi Coptic Papyrus Manuscript: a Paschal Lectionary?" *New Testament Studies*, 8 (October, 1961), pp. 70–72.

28. Allen Cabaniss, *Amalarius of Metz* (Amsterdam: North-Holland Publishing Co., 1954). Cf. also Cabaniss, *Agobard of Lyons: Churchman and Critic* (Syracuse: Syracuse University Press, 1953); and "Florus of Lyons," *Classica et Mediaevalia*, Fasc. 1–2 (1958), pp. 212–32. Both men were bitter enemies of Amalarius and his method.

29. Cabaniss, *Amalarius of Metz*, p. 64.

30. See Karl Young, *The Drama of the Medieval Church* (Oxford: Clarendon, 1933), I, 1–111.

31. O. B. Hardison, Jr., *Christian Rite and Christian Drama in the Middle Ages* (Baltimore: Johns Hopkins Press, 1965); see also Erich Auerbach, *Mimesis*, trans. W. Trask (Princeton: Princeton University Press, 1953).

32. Gustave Reese, *Music in the Middle Ages* (New York: Norton, 1940); and *Music in the Renaissance*, rev. ed. (New York: Norton, 1959); Eric Werner, *The Sacred Bridge* (New York: Columbia University Press, 1959).

33. Yrjö Hirn, *The Sacred Shrine* (London: Macmillan, 1912); Adolph Franz, *Die Messe im Deutschen Mittelalter* (Darmstadt: Wissenschaftliche Buchgesellschaft, 1963; originally published in 1902).

34. One need only recall reasons advanced for recent proclamation of the doctrine of the Assumption of the Blessed Virgin Mary.

35. Henry Adams, *Mont-Saint-Michel and Chartres* (New York: Houghton Mifflin, 1933; originally published in 1905); Otto G. von Simson, *Sacred Fortress* (Chicago: University of Chicago Press, 1948).

36. For example, coronation ceremonies, use of excommunication, the ancient reading of diptychs at Mass, Charlemagne's need for uniformity of liturgy to insure unity of his realm, etc.

37. The rituals of Freemasonry, especially in its Templar and "Scottish" degrees.

1. THE WORSHIP OF "MOST PRIMITIVE" CHRISTIANITY

1. Allen Cabaniss, "Wisdom 18:14f.: An Early Christmas Text," *Vigiliae Christianae*, 10 (July, 1956), pp. 97–102, reprinted above, pp. 53–57, "Our Lady of the Apocalypse," *Oxford Essays*, No. 1 (Oxford, Miss., 1954), *passim*.

2. Jean Daniélou, *Bible et Liturgie* (Paris: Les Editions du Cerf, 1951), pp. 84f., 90f.

3. This word was early felt to be too strong and in some MSS there is a substitution meaning "proscribed."

4. Oscar Cullman, *Early Christian Worship*, trans. A. S. Todd and J. B. Torrance (London: SCM Press, 1954), pp. 12f.

5. Ignatius, *Ephesians*, xx, 2.

6. Cf. I Cor. 12:3 and elsewhere for the context of worship.

General Note. Let me clarify a point that may be misunderstood. I am quite well aware, as all who read should be, that I am pressing words for all they are worth. I know that there are alternative interpretations, but I am concerned only with presenting my own. Let the reader therefore be ever mindful of the proverb, "Caveat emptor."

2. EARLY CHRISTIAN NIGHTTIME WORSHIP

1. I Thess. 5:6–8 and Rom. 13:12–14; cf. I Peter 5:8.

2. I Cor. 11.

3. Mark 14:22–24; Matt. 26:26–29; Luke 22:17–20.
4. John 3:1–21.
5. Matt. 28:14.
6. Luke 24:13–35.
7. John 21:4.
8. Luke 24:36–49.
9. Acts 12.
10. Acts 16:25, 33, etc.
11. Acts 20.
12. Acts 5:19.
13. Acts 23:11; 27:23f.
14. Acts 27:33–35.
15. F. L. Cross, *I Peter: A Paschal Liturgy* (London: Mowbray, 1954), passim. *Per contra,* cf. Robert H. Gundry, " 'Verba Christi' in I Peter: Their Implications Concerning the Authorship of I Peter and the Authenticity of the Gospel Tradition," *New Testament Studies,* 13 (July, 1967), pp. 336–50. Gundry's arbitrary declaration (p. 337, n. 1) that "the earlier the epistle, the less likely it reflects a highly developed . . . liturgy," is a remarkable instance of *circulus in demonstrando.* It could just as well be that by an earlier dating I Peter becomes evidence of a much earlier highly developed liturgy.

16. Allen Cabaniss, "A Note on the Liturgy of the Apocalypse," *Interpretation,* 7 (January, 1953), pp. 78–86, reprinted above, pp. 42–52, cf. also Massey H. Shepherd, Jr., *The Paschal Liturgy and the Apocalypse,* Ecumenical Studies in Worship, No. 6 (Richmond: John Knox Press, 1960).

17. Pliny, *Letters,* x, 96, on which see Cabaniss, "A Note," and "The Harrowing of Hell, Psalm 24, and Pliny the Younger: A Note," *Vigiliae Christianae,* 7 (April, 1953), pp. 65–74, reprinted above, pp. 62–71.

18. Tertullian, *Apologeticus,* vii, 1.

19. Minucius Felix, *Octavius,* viii, 3–x, 2.

20. Marcus Aurelius, *Eis heauton,* iii, 16.

21. Matt. 6:11; Luke 11:3; cf. Joachim Jeremias, *The Lord's Prayer,* trans. John Reumann, Facet Books Biblical Series, No. 8 (Philadelphia: Fortress Press, 1964), esp. pp. 23–27.

22. By "regular" services I mean the daily, weekly, or month-

ly services, not the great seasonal, semiannual, or annual occasions.

23. I Cor. 1:26.

24. John 9:4.

25. Cf. Acts 9:25; 17:10; 23:23.

26. I Thess. 5:2.

27. See, for example, J. Jeremias, *The Eucharistic Words of Jesus*, trans. A. Ehrhardt (New York: Macmillan, 1955), p. 138, esp. n. 4.

28. Mark 13:35f. Here I have fused the RSV and Knox translations.

29. Esp. Matt. 25:6.

30. Rev. 22:5; cf. 21:25.

31. II Pet. 1:19. On this verse see J. Smit Sibinga, "Une citation du Cantique dans la Secunda Petri," *Revue Biblique*, 73 (1966), pp. 107–18.

32. Cf. Luke 6:12 and many other places.

33. Cf. Matt. 14:25; John 21:4; etc.

34. Luke 2:8, 11.

35. Matt. 2:14.

36. Wisd. 16:14f. This verse is the Introit of Mass for the Sunday within the Octave of Christmas if it falls on Dec. 29, 30, or 31, the antiphon on *Magnificat* at first Vespers of that observance, the Introit of Mass for the Vigil of Epiphany, and the antiphon on *Benedictus* at Lauds on that day. These usages are examples of the beautiful artistry in the compostion of the liturgy. Wrenched from its context, where the "almighty Word" is the dread Destroying Angel slaying the Egyptian first-born on the night of the exodus, the same phrase is made to serve as an epithet of the newborn Incarnate Word. How this change was accomplished is the subject of Cabaniss, "Wisdom 18:14f.: An Early Christmas Text," *Vigiliae Christianae*, 10 (July, 1956), pp. 97–102, reprinted above, pp. 53–57.

37. There were, of course, pagan nighttime ceremonies, but their influence on Christianity was small.

38. H. St. J. Thackeray, *The Septuagint and Jewish Worship*, 2nd ed. (London: Oxford University Press, 1923), pp. 63f.;

T. H. Gaster, *Festivals of the Jewish Year* (New York: Sloane Associates, 1953), pp. 82f.

39. John 18:12.

40. Cf. the suggestive chapter on the feast of Tabernacles in J. Daniélou, *Bible et Liturgie* (Paris: Editions du Cerf, 1951); P. Carrington, *The Primitive Christian Calendar*, vol. 1, Introduction and Text (Cambridge University Press, 1952).

41. The traditional Easter Vigil may be read in any edition of *Missale Romanum*. For current popular practice, see G. L. Diekmann, ed., *The Easter Vigil Arranged for Use in Parishes* (Collegeville, Minn.: Liturgical Press, 1953).

42. Amalarius, *Liber officialis*, iii, 38.

43. Sidonius Apollinaris, *Epistolae*, v, 17.

Additional Note. O. Cullman, *Early Christian Worship*, trans. A. S. Todd and J. B. Torrance (London: SCM Press, 1954), pp. 10–12, has a discussion of the time of early Christian worship in the sense of day of the week, but not of time of the day.

3. A FRESH EXEGESIS OF MARK 2:1–12

Although I have taken the liberty of omitting elaborate documentation, I cannot refrain from mentioning four of the later publications in this field: Oscar Cullmann, *Les sacrements dans l'évangile johannique* (Paris: Presses Universitaires de France, 1951) and *Le culte dans l'église primitive*, 2nd ed. (Neuchâtel/Paris: Editions Delachaux et Niestlé, 1953); Jean Daniélou, *Bible et Liturgie* (Paris: Editions du Cerf, 1951); Philip Carrington, *The Primitive Christian Calendar*, vol. 1, Introduction and Text (Cambridge University Press, 1952). It has been said that H. St. J. Thackeray, *The Septuagint and Jewish Worship* (London: Oxford University Press for the British Academy, 1921), was the first to urge the liturgical interpretation of Scripture.

I am not blind to two weak links in my argument. (1) I cannot satisfactorily explain the presence of the scribes in the inner circle, unless perhaps they symbolize (as I have intimated above) the element of scepticism that remains in all believers. (2) Nor can I explain the significance of the paralytic himself, unless, as I have implied, he stands for the totality of the inner group. I do not believe, however, that these minor difficulties invalidate my general treatment.

4. A NOTE ON THE LITURGY OF THE APOCALYPSE

1. Pliny, *Letters*, x, 96. I have used the letter as given in *Latin Selections: Specimens of Latin Literature*, ed. E. H. Smith, rev. W. K. Clement (Boston and Chicago: Allyn and Bacon, 1891), pp. 365–67.

2. G. G. Coulton, *Medieval Panorama* (Cambridge: Cambridge University Press, 1930), pp. 14f. A. D. Nock in his important study, *Conversion* (New York: Oxford University Press, 1933), does not give sufficient weight to the external appeal of the Christian liturgy as the letter of Pliny seems to imply.

3. See my paper, "Liturgy-Making Factors in Primitive Christianity," *Journal of Religion*, 23 (January, 1943), pp. 43–58, and the appropriate citations there mentioned. Otto A. Piper, "The Apocalypse of John and the Liturgy of the Ancient Church," *Church History*, 20 (March, 1951), pp. 10–22, deals not with the form of the liturgy but with certain ideas in the Revelation that were developed in the later liturgies. There is an excellent paper by Lucetta Mowry, "Revelation 4–5 and Early Christian Liturgical Usage," *Journal of Biblical Literature*, 71, part II (June, 1952), pp. 75–84, but it shows no familiarity with the historic Christian liturgies. Massey H. Shepherd, Jr., *The Paschal Liturgy and the Apocalypse*, Ecumenical Studies in Worship, No. 6 (Richmond: John Knox Press, 1960), although seven years later than the original date of publication of my article here reprinted, overlooks it entirely.

4. Justin's *Apology* is readily available in several editions and translations. I have made use of the edition printed in J. P. Migne, *Patrologiae cursus completus: series Graeca*, vol. 6. Chapters 65–67 of the *Apology* are the ones that deal with the liturgy.

5. Justin, *Apology*, book 1, chap. 65 (the postbaptismal Eucharist); chap. 67 (the weekly Eucharist).

6. The word translated *president* is *proestos*, the one who stands up in front of the people facing them.

7. Eph. 5:19; James 5:13; and elsewhere. Pliny's phrase is, "carmenque Christo, quasi deo, dicere secum invicem...."

8. Acts 2:42.

9. See Rev. 7:2. All references in the text are to Rev. 4 and 5 unless otherwise specified, as here.

10. Ezek. 1:5–10; Isa. 6:2f. For another view, see Raymond R. Brewer, "The Influence of Greek Drama on the Apocalypse of John," *Anglican Theological Review*, 18 (April, 1936), pp. 74–92.

11. I have used the Greek text of Ignatius, *Epistles*, as given in K. Lake, ed. and trans., *The Apostolic Fathers*, Loeb Classical Library, vol. I (London: Heinemann, 1930). The references here are to *Magnesians*, vi, 1; *Trallians*, iii, 1; and *Smyrnaeans*, viii.

12. *Apology*, book 1, chaps. 65, 67.

13. For the edition of Clement, see Loeb Classical Library citation in note 11 above. The quotation here is from *Corinthians*, I, xl, 5.

14. For the altar, see Rev. 6:9–11; 8:3–5.

15. Pliny's words are *ante lucem*.

16. *Smyrnaeans*, viii.

17. *Apology*, book 1, chap. 65.

18. The Greek text of the *Didache* is also given in the Loeb Classical Library citation in note 11 above. The reference here is to *Didache*, 7.

19. Pliny: "seque sacramento non in scelus aliquod obstringere, sed ne furta, ne latrocinia, ne adulteria committerent, ne fidem fallerent, ne depositum appellati abnegarent..."

20. Ignatius, *Magnesians*, vii, 2; *Romans*, ii, 2; *Philadelphians*, iv.

21. Rev. 6:9–11; 16:7; 20:4.

22. Ibid.

23. Rev. 7:4–8; 14:1–5.

24. Rev. 7:9–12.

25. *Corinthians*, I, xl, 1.

26. *Ephesians*, iv, 1f.

27. Compare Rev. 1:10 (reference to "the Lord's day") with 1:18 (reference to the Lord's resurrection); *Didache*, xiv, 1; Ignatius, *Magnesians*, ix, 1; Pliny: "quod essent soliti stato die ante lucem convenire...."; Justin, *Apology*, book 1, chap. 67 (bis). But consult Wilfrid Stott, "A note on the word

KYPIAKH in Rev. i. 10," *New Testament Studies*, 12 (October, 1965), pp. 70–75, and K. A. Strand, "Another Look at 'Lord's Day' in the Early Church and in Rev. i. 10," *ibid.*, 13 (January, 1967), pp. 174–81.

28. *Per contra*, see Piper, "Apocalypse of John," who is certain that the "book" is the Old Testament, although he makes no effort to prove his point. I think that Mowry, "Revelation 4–5," pp. 82f., has perhaps demonstrated that the scroll is the Torah or the Deuteronomic portion of it.

29. *Apology*, book 1, chap. 67.

30. Rev. 8:3–5.

31. *Apology*, book 1, chaps. 65, 67.

32. The liturgical portion of the *Apostolic Constitutions* occurs in book 8. I have used the Greek text of Hans Lietzmann, ed., *Die Klementinische Liturgie*, Liturgische Texte, 6 (Bonn: Marcus und Weber, 1910).

33. Rev. 6:1, 3, 5, 7; 7:9–17; 8:3–5; 9:11–16, 21; 10; 14:1–5, 14–16; 15; 19:1, 4; 20:4, 11f.

34. Rev. 19:9 (supper); 21:6 (thirst); 22:2 (fruit); 22:17 (thirst, drink).

35. *Ephesians*, xx, 2.

36. *Didache*, ix, 5.

37. Some texts of Pliny read that one Christian had apostatized 20 years earlier, i. e., ca. 93; others read 25, i. e., ca. 88. The passage concerning the food is: "rursusque coeundi ad capiendum, promiscuum tamen, et innoxium. . . ." The late Dean S. E. Stout, who was preparing a new edition of Pliny's letters, assured me that the correct reading indicated that the renegade Christian had apostatized only 20 years earlier.

38. *Apology*, book 1, chap. 66.

39. The word *secret* for this prayer may be derived from *secernere* in its meaning to separate, but that is by no means proven.

40. An illustration of this in the word *Alleluia* (preserved by the New Testament church only in the book of Revelation) is presented in my note. "Alleluia: A Word and Its Effect," *Studies in English*, 5 (1964), pp. 67–74, reprinted above, pp. 114–121.

5. WISDOM 18:14-15: AN EARLY CHRISTMAS TEXT

1. *Missale Romanum* (New York: Benziger Bros., 1942), p. 26. The Vulgate text of Wisdom has *Cum enim quietum* for *Dum medium, contineret* for *tenerent, de caelo* for *de caelis,* and *prosilivit* for *venit.* It omits *Domine.* The text of the anti-phon (see note 4 below) has *perageret* for *haberet;* it omits *de caelis* and adds *alleluja* at the end. I have cited the liturgical Latin, but my analysis is, of course, based on the Greek texts of Wisdom and Ignatius.

2. *The People's Anglican Missal,* American ed. (Long Island, N. Y.: Frank Gavin Liturgical Foundation, 1946), A 29, A 37.

3. *Missale Romanum,* p. 35.

4. *Breviarium Monasticum,* Pars Prima, 3rd ed. (Bruges: Desclée, De Brouwer, 1941), pp. 286, 319.

5. J. M. Hanssens, ed., *Amalarii episcopi opera liturgica omnia,* vol. 3 (Studi e Testi, 140; Città del Vaticano: Biblioteca Apostolica Vaticana, 1950), pp. 110, 164.

6. Wisd. 18:10, LXX.

7. Wisd. 18:15-18.

8. For example, see Gregory Dix, *The Shape of the Liturgy,* 2nd ed. reprinted (Westminster: Dacre Press, 1947), p. 357 and *passim;* L. Duchesne, *Christian Worship,* trans. M. L. McClure, 5th ed. (London: SPCK, 1949), pp. 257-65a.

9. Matt. 1:18-2:12; Luke 1:26-56; 2:1-20.

10. Philip Carrington, *The Primitive Christian Calendar,* vol. 1, Introduction and Text (Cambridge University Press, 1952). Still further see my paper, "Christmas Echoes at Paschaltide," *New Testament Studies,* 9 (October, 1962), pp. 67-69, reprinted above, pp. 58-61.

11. B. J. LeFrois, *The Woman Clothed With the Sun* (Rome: 'Orbis Catholicus,' 1954); Allen Cabaniss, "Our Lady of the Apocalypse," Oxford Essays, No. 1 (Oxford, Miss., 1954).

12. The liturgical character of the Apocalypse, often recognized, is discussed by Cabaniss, "A Note on the Liturgy of the Apocalypse," *Interpretation,* 7 (January, 1953), pp. 78-86, reprinted above, pp. 42-52.

13. Tit. 3:4; cf. 2:11.

14. Heb. 10:5–7.
15. I Tim. 3:16.
16. M. R. James, trans. and ed., *The Apocryphal New Testament* (Oxford: Clarendon, 1950), pp. 38–49.
17. LeFrois, *The Woman*, pp. 39–41, discusses and discourages the theory that the passage from Ignatius may be a *direct* allusion to Rev. 12.
18. Wisd. 18:14; Ignatius, *Ephesians*, xix, 1.
19. Wisd. 18:17; Ign., *Eph.*, xix, 2.
20. Wisd. 18:19; Ign., *Eph.*, xix, 3.
21. Wisd. 18:3; Ign., *Eph.*, xix, 2.
22. Wisd. 18:15 *(ap' ouranon)* and Ign., *Eph.*, xix, 2 *(en ouranoi);* Wisd. 18:1, 4 *(megiston . . . phos)* and Ign., *Eph.*, xix, 2 *(phos autou);* Wisd. 18:3 *(helion)* and Ign., *Eph.*, xix, 2 *(helioi);* Wisd. 18:15 *(thronon basileion)* and Ign., *Eph.*, xix, 3 *(palaia basileia);* Wisd. 18:16 *(thanatou)* and Ign., *Eph.*, xix, 3 *(thanatou).*
23. Wisd. 18:1–4.
24. Wisd. 18:5.
25. Wisd. 18:9.
26. Wisd. 18:13.
27. Ign., *Eph.*, xix, 1.
28. Wisd. 18:14.
29. Ibid.
30. Wisd. 18:15.
31. Wisd. 18:17.
32. Ign., *Eph.*, xix, 2.
33. Wisd. 18:10.
34. Wisd. 18:13.
35. Wisd. 18:11f., 16, 18.
36. Wisd. 18:17.
37. Ign., *Eph.*, xix, 3.
38. If we may regard this relation between Wisd. 18 and Ign., *Eph.*, xix, as probable, then we must face the possibility that Rev. 12 may, after all, be a still earlier indication of the Christmas application of Wisd. 18:14f. and thus *indirectly* alluded to by Ignatius (see note 17 above). Rev. 12 is certainly an ornate version of the Nativity narrative; it too records an initial hiddenness, then a manifestation, and the subsequent results, as

do both Wisd. 18 and Ign., *Eph.*, xix; and it furnishes some verbal parallels mentioned by LeFrois.

39. Dix, *Shape of the Liturgy*, p. 456, n. 1, states: "It is hardly necessary to refute the assertion of the same authority [the *Liber Pontificalis*] that Pope Telesphorus (martyred *ca.* A.D. 130) 'ordained that before the sacrifice the Angels' hymn . . . should be said but only on Christmas at night. . . .' The festival of Christmas did not exist until, at the earliest, a century and a half after Telesphorus." In view of the argument presented above, I suggest as a tentative alternative to Dix's statement that the account of Pope Telesphorus preserves a true tradition and may be cited as confirmation of my proposal. Dix's last sentence is surely correct only if by it he means that a universally accepted date, Dec. 25, Jan. 6, or some other, was not fixed as Christmas until the third or fourth century.

See also the version of *Liber Pontificalis* by L. R. Loomis, trans. and ed., *The Book of the Popes* (New York: Columbia University Press, 1916), 1:13, n. 1: "The night mass at Christmas . . . can hardly have been instituted before the date of the Nativity was fixed during the fourth century." This remark is a non sequitur: elsewhere [see my paper, "Early Christian Nighttime Worship," *Journal of Bible and Religion*, 25 (January, 1957), pp. 30–33, reprinted above, pp. 30–36] I have demonstrated that Mass at night was customary virtually from the beginning of Christianity, without respect of the occasion. Regardless, then, of the date of Christmas, and even if it were an erratically variable festival, a night Mass was normal by the end of the first century.

I believe that I have also met the argument so ably and beautifully presented by Oscar Cullman, "The Origin of Christmas," in his compilation, *The Early Church*, ed. by A. J. B. Higgins (Philadelphia: Westminster Press, 1956), pp. 21–36.

Additional Note. I am assured by Professor Samuel Sandmel of the Hebrew Union College, Cincinnati, Ohio, that there is "no evidence at all that the passage was ever used out of context by any Jewish Messianist." The fact, of course, confirms the essential artistic genius of the unknown Christian who first removed Wisdom 18:14f. from its context and gave it a new and beautiful meaning by associating it with the Incarnation.

6. CHRISTMAS ECHOES AT PASCHALTIDE

1. See especially John A. T. Robinson, "Elijah, John and Jesus: An Essay in Detection," *New Testament Studies*, 4 (July, 1958), pp. 263–81, in particular p. 279, n. 2, and the literature therein cited. This essay is now available in Robinson, *Twelve New Testament Studies*, Studies in Biblical Theology, No. 14 (Naperville, Ill.: Alec R. Allenson, Inc., 1962), pp. 28–52.

2. On the antiquity of celebration of Christmas, see my note, "Wisdom 18:14f.: An Early Christmas Text," *Vigiliae Christianae*, 10 (July, 1956), pp. 97–102, reprinted above, pp. 53–57.

7. THE HARROWING OF HELL, PSALM 24, AND PLINY THE YOUNGER: A NOTE

1. See, for example, W. H. Hulme, *The Middle-English Harrowing of Hell and Gospel of Nicodemus*, Early English Text Society, Extra Series, No. 100 (London: Kegan Paul, Trench, Trubner and Co., 1907), *passim* and the literature therein cited.

2. M. R. James, *The Apocryphal New Testament* (Oxford: Clarendon Press, 1950), pp. 94f., 117–46; J. A. MacCulloch, *The Harrowing of Hell* (Edinburgh: T. and T. Clark, 1930), *passim*, but esp. pp. 152–73. Since MacCulloch's excellent treatise is extensively documented, I believe that no end will be served by burdening my brief paper with numerous bibliographical references. Furthermore, dogmatic considerations are not my purpose in this essay. My concern is to present a two-fold hypothesis: first, to account for the liturgical association of Psalm 24 with the *descensus* doctrine; and, second, to interpret Pliny's letter tentatively as literary evidence of that association.

3. Col. 1:18; I Cor. 15:20.

4. Hos. 13:14; Isa. 25:8.

5. Isa. 42:7; cf. I Pet. 3:19, notably the reference to prison.

6. Isa. 42:7; cf. I Pet. 3:19, but see also Isa. 24:22; 26:19; 59:10; Ps. 30:3; 107:10, 14; 143:3.

7. Ps. 6:5; 30:9; 88:10–12; 115:17; Eccl. 9:10; Isa. 29:4; 38:18.

8. Eccl. 3:19f.; 9:2–6.
9. Dan. 12:2f.; II Esd. 2:45; II Macc. 12:43–45.
10. II Sam. 12:23; Job 14:10–12; 17:13–16; Eccl. 12:5, 7.
11. Job 19:25–27; Isa. 26:19; Ezek. 37:12–14; Dan. 12:2f.;
Song of the Three Children 66; II Macc. 7:14; 12:43.
12. Ps. 116:15; 139:7–10; Prov. 15:11; Wisd. 3:1–3.
13. II Tim. 1:10; John 1:5.
14. Ps. 107:14; I Pet. 3:19.
15. I Cor. 15:52.
16. Matt. 25:46; 27:52; Luke 16:22–26; I Pet. 4:6; II Pet. 2:4.
17. Rom. 6:8; I Cor. 15:52–57; II Tim. 1:10.
18. Rom. 14:8f.; Rev. 1:18.
19. Solomon B. Freehof, *The Book of Psalms: A Commentary* (Cincinnati: Union of American Hebrew Congregations, 1938), pp. 61–64, esp. p. 61, citing the Mishnah (Tamid, vii, 4) for the list of Proper Psalms for each day of the week. See also Suitbert Bäumer, *Historie du Bréviaire*, trans. from German into French by Réginald Biron (Paris: Letouzey et Ané, 1905), 1: 52, where there is also a reference to the same Mishnah passage.
20. Ps. 107:16; Isa. 45:1f.
21. Ex. 40:34; I Kings 8:11.
22. John 12:31; 14:30; 16:11; I Cor. 2:6; Eph. 2:2; cf. Eph. 6:12.
23. Pliny, *Letters*, x, 96. Although he did not fully agree with my interpretation, I am greatly indebted to the late Dean S. E. Stout, Indiana University, for valuable comments on the text of this famous letter. Dean Stout was engaged in preparing a new edition of Pliny.
24. See the distinction made in Eph. 5:19.
25. I say four details instead of five because thievery and banditry differ only in degree, not in kind; whereas adultery, lying, and violation of trust differ in kind from one another and from thievery and banditry. Furthermore, there seems to be here an echo of the last four commandments of the Decalogue (Protestant enumeration), which are concerned with stealing, committing adultery, bearing false witness, and coveting.
26. Cf. Matt. 5:28.
27. Cf. Ps. 15:4. I am aware that there is no precise verbal

parallel between Pliny's statement and Ps. 24:4, but the ideas are strikingly similar. We must remember that we are dealing with a contemptuous pagan's analysis based on a report made by apostates, and hence we cannot expect much more than a general agreement. Yet under the circumstances, the parallel is quite impressive.

28. Justin Martyr, *Dialogue with Trypho* (*ca.* 150), xxvi, quotes the entire Psalm as a prophetic parable of Christ as God and as Lord of hosts. Verses 7–10 are applied to the Resurrection and Ascension together as an appeal to the gates of heaven to open, since Christ, still bearing the marks of crucifixion, was not immediately recognizable to the guardians of the celestial gates. Irenaeus, *Against Heresies* (*ca.* 185), xxxiii, 13, also binding together the Death, Resurrection, and Ascension of the Lord, considers these verses as an appeal for the opening of the gates of heaven. Tertullian, *On Flight in Persecution* (*ca.* 200), xii, connects the Psalm with the Harrowing. For a description of the rite of dedication of a church, see Louis Duchesne, *Christian Worship: Its Origin and Development*, English trans. by M. L. McClure, 5th ed., reprinted (London: SPCK, 1949), pp. 399–418.

29. Gregory Dix, *The Shape of the Liturgy*, 2nd ed., 3rd impression (Westminster: Dacre Press, 1947), pp. 349, 351, and *passim*.

30. See an excellent discussion by Louis Bouyer, *The Paschal Mystery*, English trans. by Sister Mary Benoit (Chicago: Henry Regnery Co., 1950), pp. 97–105, esp. pp. 103f.

Additional Note. I should perhaps add two further bibliographical notices: Franz Cumont, *Lux Perpetua* (Paris: Librairie Orientaliste Paul Geuthner, 1949), passim, esp. p. 234; and R. M. Grant, "Pliny and the Christians," *Harvard Theological Review*, 41 (October, 1948), pp. 273f. Although an interesting analysis, the latter in no way affects my interpretation.

Since original publication of my foregoing article, there has appeared a fine study by R. P. Martin, *Carmen Christi* (Cambridge: Cambridge University Press, 1967). He deals with the Pliny passage on pp. 1–9, but makes no reference to my paper or to some of the bibliography therein cited. His presentation contains nothing to require any change in my treatment.

8. PETRONIUS AND THE GOSPEL BEFORE THE GOSPELS?

a. A Footnote to the "Petronian Question"

1. F. Bücheler, *Petronii Satirae*, 5th ed. (Berlin, 1911); this story occurs in secs. 111f. A brief bibliography concerning the story is given by E. V. Marmorale, *La Questione Petroniana* (Bari, 1948), p. 120, n. 45. On the "Milesian tale," see the note by W. B. Sedgwick, *Cena Trimalchionis* . . ., 2nd ed. (Oxford, 1950), p. 141. The relevant Biblical materials are Matt. 27:57–28:15; Mark 15:42–16:8; Luke 23:50–24:12; and John 19:38–20:12.

2. The rock-hewn sepulcher *(mnemeion, taphos, mnema)* is mentioned by all four Gospels; proximity to the place of crucifixion is explicitly stated by John, implied by the other three.

3. The criminals crucified with Christ are called "robbers" *(lestai)* in Matt. 27:38 and Mark 15:27. Pilate is identified in the Matthean record as *hegemon;* see Matt. 27:2, 14, 15, 21; 28:14. Note also Luke 3:1, where derivatives of this word are used of both emperor and procurator: "In the fifteenth year of the reign *(hegemonias)* of Tiberius Caesar, Pontius Pilate being governor *(hegemoneuontos)* of Judaea. . . ." Cf. the language of Tacitus, *Annals*, 15. 44: "auctor nominis eius Christus Tiberio imperitante per procuratorem Pontium Pilatum supplicio adfectus erat. . . ." The wording of Luke 3:1 shows that Marmorale *La Questione*, p. 100) is clearly in error when he states so emphatically: l *'imperator provinciae* nel senso di proconsule, o di propretore nel caso di provincie imperiali, non si trova mai al tempo dell 'impero, e se ne comprende la ragione; si trova invece negli scrittori del periodo repubblicano, o in scrittori che narrano cose di quel periodo." See especially the evidence in J. H. Moulton and G. Milligan, *The Vocabulary of the Greek Testament*, reprinted (Grand Rapids, Mich., 1950), p. 277, s. v. *hegemon.*

4. Two women only (Mary Magdalene and the "other" Mary) are mentioned in Matt. 27:61; 28:1; Mark 15:47 (in 16:1 there is added, "and Salome"). Luke 23:55 says indefinitely,

"the women," and does not identify them until late in the Resurrection story (24:10).

5. Possibility of theft of the body of Christ, not indeed from the cross, but from His burial place, and the need for a guard to watch the tomb are alluded to at length in Matt. 27:62–66; 28:4, 11–15.

6. Light shining amid the gloom of the sepulchers is suggested in Matt. 28:3 and Luke 24:4, but these parallels are hardly fair.

7. Guards' fear of supernatural apparition—Matt. 28:4; women's fear—Mark 16:8; Luke 24:5.

8. Cf. note 5 above.

9. Cf. similar account of a Philippian jailor, Acts 16:27.

10. Rom. 16:12. Cf. also the (apocryphal) *Acts of Paul*, ii. 7–43, esp. 27–41. The locale of the romance of Saints Paul and Thecla (written *ca.* 160) is the Asia Minor town of Iconium, where a wealthy queen named Tryphaena made herself the protector of Thecla. See M. R. James, trans. and annot., *The Apocryphal New Testament* (Oxford, 1926), pp. 272–81. There was a historical Queen Tryphaena, widow of King Cotys of Thrace, mother of King Polemo II of Pontus, and great-niece of the Emperor Claudius. For etymological reasons, if no other, Tryphaena ("Dainty") was a name common enough in the Mediterranean world.

11. The nine-day period of the Milesian tale is deduced as follows: the crucifixions were performed on the fifth day of the matron's vigil; the assignations were kept during that night and the two following; then the soldier brought presents for the widow and carried them to the vault at nightfall (of what seems to be the fourth night of assignation); the empty cross was observed the next day, the ninth after the initiation of the woman's vigil. The approximately nine- or ten-day interval between the ascension and Pentecost is based on the fact that Pentecost was the fiftieth day after Passover and on the tradition that Christ remained on earth after His resurrection for forty days; cf. Acts 1:3, 15; 2:1.

12. Not significant is the sentence from *Satiricon* 74: "haec dicente eo gallus gallinaceus cantavit." But cf. Luke 22:60:

"while he was still speaking, a cock crowed." (See below where I have reversed my opinion about this matter.)

13. *Satiricon* 102.

14. Poem 97, attributed to Petronius by E. Baehrens, *Poetae Latini minores* (Leipzig, 1882), 4: 98.

15. M. Simon, *Verus Israel: Étude sur les Relations entre Chrétiens et Juifs dans l'Empire Romain 135-425* (Paris, 1948), pp. 125-62; S. G. F. Brandon, *The Fall of Jerusalem and the Christian Church* (London, 1951), pp. 88-121, 126-53.

16. Presumably not hitherto noticed. Even stranger, however, is the fact that no Pauline commentary (to my knowledge) mentions the Petronian Tryphaena in connection with Rom. 16:12. Cf. W. Sanday and A. C. Headlam, *A Critical and Exegetical Commentary on the Epistle to the Romans* (New York, 1896, and often reprinted).

17. Marmorale, *La Questione*, is the latest, embodying notices of a great many previous studies; as one reviewer (Van Buren; see note 19 below) has said, it in part supersedes earlier treatises and "may well serve as a starting-point for future investigators." I shall add here only two other references for the sake of their bibliographies: A. Collignon, *Étude sur Pétrone* (Paris, 1892); E. T. Sage, ed., *Petronius: The Satiricon* (New York, 1929), a compact, useful, trustworthy edition despite its age and its publication as a textbook. For an altogether delightful summary and appreciative discussion of the *Satiricon*, see the third lecture in F. A. Todd, *Some Ancient Novels* (Oxford, 1940); cf. also the perceptive remarks by E. Auerbach, *Mimesis: Dargestellte Wirklichkeit in der Abendländischen Literatur* (Bern, 1946), pp. 31-55.

18. Tacitus, *Annals*, 16. 17-20, esp. 18f.

19. The learned Marmorale is the leading exponent of the later date. Only a sampling of reviews of his very thorough *La Questione Petroniana* (the result of many years of study and a complete reversal of his former, the traditional, opinion) can be given here. E. E. Burriss (now deceased), *American Journal of Philology*, 71 (1950), pp. 327-31, was completely convinced by Marmorale's presentation, although he indicated a minor flaw in the argument against water clocks on public display during the time of Nero. A. W. Van Buren, *Journal of Roman*

Studies, 39 (1949), pp. 201f., was also favorable, considering some of the argumentation irrefutable. Joshua Whatmough, *Classical Philology,* 44 (1949), pp. 273f., in a whimsical and flippant review, remained unconvinced, stating: "Unless some lucky find of a more positive character should turn up to prove his contention, the accepted date and authorship are likely to remain in favor. It is, nevertheless, fitting to have been reminded that they are only presumptive, not proved." F. de Ruyt, *Études classiques,* 18 (1949), pp. 427f., in a fair and judicious review, clung to the traditional view, feeling that Marmorale was sincere but filled with the ardor of a "convert." A. Maniet, too, *Antiquité classique,* 18 (1949), pp. 450–53, remained of the older opinion, although he recognized and paid tribute to Marmorale's scholarship and integrity.

20. Cf. note 15 above.

21. Marcion fl. *ca.* 160. See note 10 above for Tryphaena.

22. J. P. Postgate, *Phaedri fabulae Aesopiae* (Oxford, 1919), *Appendix Perottina* 13: "Mulier vidua et miles" (the attribution to Phaedrus is not certain). Phaedrus may have been born *ca.* 15 B.C. Both versions are translated, analyzed, and compared below.

23. See note 15 above, esp. Simon, *Verus Israel,* pp. 82–93; Brandon, *The Fall,* pp. 74–87. Cf. the fragment of Tacitus' history preserved in Sulpicius Severus (*Historia sacra,* 2. 30. 6): the Emperor Titus hoped to overthrow both Judaism and Christianity by demolishing the Temple in A.D. 70; these religions, although differing in part, came from the same sources, the Christians from the Jews; if, therefore, the root was destroyed, the offshoot would easily perish. In C. D. Fisher, *C. Taciti historiarum libri* (Oxford, 1939), frag. 2.

24. Note such vague, general expressions as, "exitiabilis superstitio . . . .," "sed per urbem quo cuncta undique atrocia aut pudenda confluunt celebranturque . . . .," "odio humani generis . . .," and "miseratio oriebatur. . . ." (Tacitus, *Annals,* 15. 44). Cf. Matt. 28:11–15, "and this account has been spread among the Jews to this very day." The vagueness of the Tacitus chapter may be deliberate and instinctive, according to F. W. Clayton, "Tacitus and Nero's Persecution of the Christians," *Classical Quarterly,* 41 (1947), pp. 81–85. There was an oral tradition

of the disposition of Christ's body among the Jews as late as the ninth century; see Agobard (d. 840), *De Judaicis superstitionibus* (*MGH: Epistolae Karolini aevi*, 3: 185–99), and chap. 7 of my *Agobard of Lyons: Churchman and Critic* (Syracuse, N. Y., 1953). Shortly after Agobard some of these garbled accounts were reduced to writing. For whatever it is worth, there is now Hugh J. Schonfield, *The Passover Plot* (New York, 1965), which exploits to the fullest such accounts.

25. See note 3 above.
26. See note 22 above.
27. Tacitus, *Annals*, 16. 17, 18.
28. H. Leclercq, s.v. "Bithynie," in F. Cabrol and H. Leclercq, *Dictionnaire d'archéologie chrétienne et de liturgie*, 2 pt. 1 (Paris, 1925), p. 916. Cf. also Acts 16:6–8; I Pet. 1:1.
29. Pliny Minor, *Letters*, x, 96. Cf. my earlier essay in this volume, "The Harrowing of Hell, Psalm 24, and Pliny the Younger," reprinted above, pp. 62–71.
30. Since Marmorale, *La Questione*, is of such vital importance it seems necessary (to me) to add a few specific remarks about the book. It is a very thorough examination of the "question," and has, as Whatmough says (note 19 above), the "spice of novelty," but "the longer it is pondered, the more it takes a negative color." So favorable a critic as Van Buren admits (note 19 above) that many pages "fail in themselves to yield a positive result," although he hastens to say cautiously, "yet when due allowance has been made, a residuum emerges which appears to possess cogency for assigning the romance to the Late Antonine period."

Marmorale's most important chapters, 4 and 5, the discussion of the language of Petronius, are, in a manner of speaking, deceptive—unless one "counts pages." If one does that, one discovers that the longest sections are (1) the comparison with Seneca (pp. 224–35), which is precisely consonant with the traditional date rather than with the period after 180; and (2) the consideration of the linguistic particularity of the *Satiricon* (pp. 198–223), which does not compel one to feel that either date is absolutely necessary (even Van Buren similarly acknowledges that "the literary style is *sui generis*").

Moreover, the attempt to associate the immorality of the

Satiricon with the days of Commodus and Elagabalus only (pp. 310–13) ignores the testimony of Paul for the days of Nero; see Rom. 1:26f. (very strong); I Cor. 6:9; Gal. 5:19–21. Cf. also I Tim. 1:10.

In note 3 above, I called attention to too emphatic an assertion. There are others: for example, the attribution of II Tim. to Paul (p. 72) is not generally acceptable today; the evidence concerning early use of *clausulae* (p. 293, n. 11; p. 294, nn. 17, 18; p. 296, n. 20) is enthusiastically misused; and mention of a *pervigilium Priapi* in *Satiricon* 21 is correlated with the *Pervigilium Veneris*, ignoring the equally significant mention of *pervigilia* in Tacitus, *Annals*, 15. 44.

It seems to me that the weakest links in the argument are the failure to consider common-dialect Greek usage of the first century and the notion that a vast mass of multiplied comparisons will bear weight instead of falling under it. K. F. C. Rose, *The Date and Author of the Satyricon*, announced for publication in 1968, has not yet appeared.

b. The *Satiricon* and the Christian Oral Tradition

1. Allen Cabaniss, "A Footnote to the 'Petronian Question,'" *Classical Philology*, 49 (1954), pp. 98–102, reprinted above, pp. 72–77.

2. Gilbert Bagnani, *Arbiter of Elegance: A Study of the Life and Works of C. Petronius, The Phoenix*, suppl. vol. 2 (Toronto, 1954). Despite his intemperate language, I believe that Bagnani has made his case that the *Satiricon* was written by Petronius between A.D. 58 and 65. Referring to my remarks in *Classical Philology* (*supra*, note 1), Bagnani states ambiguously (p. 64, n. 71): "If these similarities are anything more than coincidences—which seems to me doubtful—Petronius may possibly have heard some vague accounts of the Crucifixion while in Bithynia." Bagnani's sentence does not lend itself to precise grammatical analysis and I cannot decide whether he agrees with me or not.

3. Philip Carrington, *The Early Christian Church, I: The First Christian Century* (Cambridge, 1957), p. 67.

4. Ibid., p. 72.

5. Ibid., pp. 130, 439f.

158   NOTES TO PAGES 78–91

6. Bagnani, *Arbiter of Elegance*, p. 48.
7. M. R. James, *The Apocryphal New Testament* (Oxford, 1950), p. 90.
8. Cabaniss, "A Footnote."
9. Cabaniss, "Early Christian Nighttime Worship," *Journal of Bible and Religion*, 25 (1957), pp. 30–33; reprinted above, pp. 30–36.

c. The Matron of Ephesus Again: An Analysis

1. Jeremy Taylor, *Holy Living and Dying* (London: H. G. Bohn, 1850), pp. 516f.
2. There is a convenient English version by Joseph B. Pike, *Frivolities of Courtiers and Footprints of Philosophers* (Minneapolis: University of Minnesota Press, 1938), pp. 361–63.
3. Eduard Grisebach, *Die Wanderung der Novelle von der treulosen Wittwe durch die Weltliteratur*, 2nd ed. (Berlin: F. and P. Lehmann, 1889), *passim*.
4. John P. Postgate, *Phaedri fabulae Aesopiae cum Nicolai Perotti prologo et decem novis fabulis* (Oxford: Clarendon Press, 1919). For the matron-of-Ephesus story, see therein *Appendix Perottina*, p. xiii. On Phaedrus and his work, consult Martin Schanz and Carl Hosius, *Geschichte der römischen Literatur* (Munich: C. H. Beck, 1935), pp. 447–56; Georg Wissowa and Wilhelm Kroll, *Paulys Real-Encyclopädie der Classischen Altertums Wissenschaft*, neue Bearbeitung (Stuttgart: J. B. Metzler, 1937), xix (2), coll. 1475–1505.
5. Evan T. Sage, *Petronius: The Satiricon* (New York: Century Co., 1929), Introduction and Notes, passim. For the matron-of-Ephesus story, see therein secs. 111f. (pp. 95–98). On Petronius and his work, consult Schanz and Hosius, *Geschichte*, pp. 509–20; Wissowa and Kroll, *Paulys*, xix (1), coll. 1201–1214.
6. Cf. Vulgate version of Mark 8:36; not noted in my papers mentioned in note 11 below.
7. Cf. Sage, *Petronius*, p. 95, line 10.
8. This enumeration may be off one day.
9. Cf. the title of Grisebach's work in note 3 above.
10. Jean Pierre Abel Remusat, *Contes chinois* (Paris: Moutardier, 1827), 3: 144–97.

11. Allen Cabaniss, "A Footnote to the 'Petronian Question,' " *Classical Philology*, 49 (April, 1954), pp. 98–102, reprinted above, pp. 72–77; "The *Satiricon* and the Christian Oral Tradition," *Greek, Roman, and Byzantine Studies*, 3 (Winter, 1960), pp. 36–39, reprinted above, pp. 77–81.

12. See Cabaniss, "A Footnote," and Hugh J. Schonfield, *According to the Hebrews* (London: Duckworth, 1937), passim.

d. The Matron of Ephesus: An Identification

1. John P. Postgate, *Phaedri fabulae Aesopiae cum Nicolai Perotti prologo et decem novis fabulis* (Oxford: Clarendon Press, 1919), *Appendix Perottina*, p. xiii; Evan T. Sage, *Petronius: The Satiricon* (New York: Century Co., 1929), pp. 95–98.

2. See, e. g., John 8:41 and similar passages for canonical evidence, and the Protevangelium (or Gospel) of James for apocryphal evidence.

3. An edition and translation of Lucian is found in the Loeb Classical Library in eight volumes. The passing of Peregrinus is presented in vol. 5 (Cambridge: Harvard University Press, 1936), pp. 2–51. Celsus, *True Discourse*, is no longer extant, but most of it is known from its incorporation into Origen's reply, *Contra Celsum*, of which a convenient translation is given in *The Ante-Nicene Fathers*, (Buffalo: Christian Literature Publishing Co., 1885), 4: 395–669.

4. See preceding note. This particular writing is given on pp. 54–99.

5. Hugh J. Schonfield, *According to the Hebrews* (London: Duckworth, 1937).

6. Allen Cabaniss, "A Footnote to the 'Petronian Question,' " *Classical Philology*, 49 (April, 1954), pp. 98–102, reprinted above, pp. 72–77; "The *Satiricon* and the Christian Oral Tradition," *Greek, Roman, and Byzantine Studies*, 3 (Winter, 1960), pp. 36–39, reprinted above, pp. 77–81.

7. Cabaniss, "The Matron of Ephesus Again: An Analysis," *Studies in English*, 2 (1961): 41–53, reprinted above, pp. 81–93.

8. Cabaniss, "Eine Quelle zu Faulkners 'Die Fabel,' " *Schweizer Monatshefte*, Heft 9, 37 Jahr (December, 1957);

English version, "A Source of Faulkner's *Fable*," *Studies in English*, 6 (1965), pp. 87–89.

9. A NOTE ON THE DATE OF THE GREAT ADVENT ANTIPHONS

1. F. Cabrol, "L'avent liturgique," *Revue Bénédictine*, 22 (1905), pp. 484–95, esp. p. 494.
2. H. Thurston, "The Great Advent Antiphons, Heralds of Christmas," *The Month*, 106 (1905), pp. 616–31.
3. Ibid., pp. 620f.
4. Ibid., p. 622.
5. F. Cabrol, "Avent," *Dictionnaire d'archéologie chrétienne et de liturgie* (Paris: Letouzey et Ané, 1907), vol. 1, col. 3229 and note.
6. Thurston, "Advent Antiphons," p. 625.
7. Boethius, *De consolatione philosophiae*, 3: 12 (prose). Italics mine. See the Loeb Classical Library edition, translation of "I. T.," revised by H. F. Stewart (Cambridge: Harvard University Press, 1936), p. 290. See also notes 11 and 12 below.
8. *Breviarium Romanum*, Pars Hiemalis (Paris: Desclée, 1912), pp. 209f. Italics mine. There is a beautiful translation for liturgical use in Winfred Douglas, *The Monastic Diurnal* (New York: Oxford University Press, 1935), p. 172.
9. Wisdom 8:1.
10. M. B. Ogle, "Bible Text or Liturgy?" *Harvard Theological Review*, 33 (1940), pp. 191–224, does not discuss this problem.
11. Boethius, *De consolatione philosophiae*, ed. Adrian Fortescue (London: Burns Oates and Washburne, 1928), p. 98n. It is surprising that "O Sapientia" did not occur immediately to the liturgiologist.
12. Boethius, *Philosophiae consolatio*, ed. W. Weinburger (Vienna: Hoelder-Pichler-Tempsky, 1934), p. 75n. Rand's remark is cited from *Jahrbuch für Philologie*, suppl. 26, p. 401, which I have not been able to consult.
13. Fortescue annotates twenty-seven passages with Scripture citations; Weinburger, eleven. The single point at which these references overlap is at the words *cuncta fortiter suaviterque disponit*. I have independently discovered nine additional

Biblical parallels. This gives a total of forty-five places, other than the words under discussion, at which Boethius might have made apt allusions.

10. *Beowulf* AND THE LITURGY

1. Fr. Klaeber, "Die christlichen Elemente im Beowulf," *Anglia*, 35 (1912; Neue Folge Band XXIII), pp. 111–36, 249–70, 453–82; 36 (1912; Neue Folge Band XXIV), pp. 169–99. See also R. W. Chambers, *Beowulf: An Introduction*, 2nd ed. (Cambridge: University Press, 1932), pp. 121–28; W. W. Lawrence, *Beowulf and Epic Tradition* (Cambridge, Mass.: Harvard University Press, 1930), pp. 281–84; Ritchie Girvan, *Beowulf and the Seventh Century* (London: Methuen, 1935).

2. For brief bibliographical references on this topic, consult my note, "The Harrowing of Hell, Psalm 24, and Pliny the Younger," *Vigiliae Christianae*, 7 (April, 1953), pp. 65–74, reprinted above, pp. 62–72.

3. Fr. Klaeber, *Beowulf and the Fight at Finnsburg*, 1st ed. (New York: Heath, 1922), p. li. I have employed Klaeber's edition for all references to the poem. Most of the references are given in parentheses in the body of the paper.

4. And especially the "Gospel of Nicodemus," 18:1f., as given in M. R. James, *The Apocryphal New Testament* (Oxford: Clarendon, 1950), p. 124f.

5. Note the very liturgical term, *nōn*, for "ninth hour."

6. Here, of course, one is reminded of Caedmon.

7. The ritual of Holy Saturday may be consulted in any edition of *Missale Romanum* and that of baptism in *Rituale Romanum*. See also Adrian Fortescue, *The Ceremonies of the Roman Rite Described*, 8th ed., rev. and aug. J. C. O'Connell (Westminster, Md.: Newman Press, 1949), *ad loc.* For historical considerations, consult L. Duchesne, *Christian Worship: Its Origin and Evolution*, trans. M. L. McClure, 5th ed. reprinted (London: SPCK, 1949), pp. 250–57, 292–338; A. Fortescue, *The Mass*, 9th impression (London: Longmans, Green, 1950); Gregory Dix, *The Shape of the Liturgy*, 3rd impression (Westminster: Dacre, 1947). Although it belongs to the tenth century, the *Regularis Concordia* has an interesting description of English

usage concerning the "new fire," especially the employment of a dragon-shaped candlestick; see Thomas Symons, ed. and trans., *Regularis Concordia* (New York: Oxford University Press, 1953), p. 39.

8. For an excellent discussion of ancient baptismal symbolism, see Jean Daniélou, *Bible et Liturgie* (Paris: Editions du Cerf, 1951), a rewarding study of the Biblical theology of the sacraments and ecclesiastical festivals as it is expressed in the Church Fathers. Since it is replete with detailed citations of Patristic sources, I shall not attempt to reiterate its documentation. The reader is urged to use this very essential work; I rely on it heavily in this paper. This type of interpretation is by no means outmoded; for an illuminating contemporary presentation of it, see L. Bouyer, *The Paschal Mystery*, trans. Sister Mary Benoit (Chicago: Regnery, 1950), a series of appealing meditations on the last three days of Holy Week. Bouyer's approach is essentially Patristic.

9. The Latin of the passage here translated is given in Duchesne, *Christian Worship*, p. 255, where it is dated late eighth century or earlier. Both Duchesne, p. 255; n. 2, and Bouyer, *Paschal Mystery*, p. 271, describe the digression as "Virgilian." That characterization may indeed be correct, but I wonder if it may be ultimately Scriptural. In the LXX version of Prov. 6:8, following the familiar passage beginning, "Go to the ant, thou sluggard; consider her ways, and be wise," there is an expansion which reads (my translation): "Or go to the bee, and learn what a worker she is, and how respectfully she does her work, whose labors kings and commoners use for their health. Desired she is and praised by all; although weak in strength, she is preferred because she has honored wisdom." Some of the Old Latin versions, following the LXX, also have this addition. See my brief note, "The Beehive Problem," *New Age*, 72 (November, 1964), pp. 21f.

10. On the etymology, see Chambers, *Beowulf*, pp. 365–69. It is by no means farfetched or improbable to suppose that mention of one thing may evoke a train of thought dealing with the precise opposite.

11. On the general plane of the relation of *Beowulf* to allegory, see J. R. R. Tolkien, "Beowulf: The Monsters and the

Critics," *Proceedings of the British Academy*, 22 (1936), pp. 245–95; T. M. Gang, "Approaches to *Beowulf*," *Review of English Studies*, 3, n.s. (January, 1952), pp. 1–12; Adrian Bonjour, "Monsters Crouching and Critics Rampant," *PMLA*, 68 (March, 1953): 304–12; A. G. Brodeur, "The Structure and the Unity of *Beowulf*," *PMLA*, 68 (December, 1953), pp. 1183–95.

12. J. W. Bright, "The Relation of the Caedmonian *Exodus* to the Liturgy," *Modern Language Notes*, 27 (April, 1912), pp. 97–103; C. W. Kennedy, *The Earliest English Poetry: A Critical Survey* (New York: Oxford University Press, 1943), pp. 175–83.

13. Cf. Kennedy, *Earliest English Poetry*, pp. 181f.; G. K. Anderson, *The Literature of the Anglo-Saxons* (Princeton: Princeton University Press, 1949), pp. 122f.

14. The Venerable Bede (died 735) does not supply any notable occasions of the administration of baptism, but he does afford record of some remarkable conversions that apparently imply use of the full ritual and ceremonial; see particularly his *Historia ecclesiastica Anglorum gentis*, 2: 13 (the famous case of King Edwin).

15. Nor do we find in the record of St. Boniface's life (died 754) any actual accounts of baptism, but we do find instances of dramatic conversion that were presumably followed by impressive baptismal ceremonies; see Willibald, *Vita Bonifatii*, 6, 9.

16. Charlemagne's query (*ca.* 810) is given in J. M. Hanssens, ed., *Amalarii episcopi opera liturgica omnia* (Studi e Testi, 138; Città del Vaticano: Biblioteca Apostolica Vaticana, 1948), 1: 235f., and the reply of Amalarius, bishop of Trèves, in ibid., pp. 236–51. A few of the other answers: Leidrad, bishop of Lyons, *De sacramento baptismi* and *Epistola II* (Migne, *Patrologia latina*, xcix, 853–72, 873–84); Jesse of Amiens, *De baptismo*, PL, cv, 781–96; Maxentius of Aquileia, *De significatu rituum baptismi*, PL, cvi, 51–54. It may be worthwhile to call attention to the elaborate portrayal of the baptism of a Danish king and queen as depicted in Book 4 of Ermoldus Nigellus, *De rebus gestis Ludovici pii*, PL, cv, 569–640, written about 826. Note especially the description of the scene of the ritual, the chapel at Ingelheim.

17. Bright, "The Relation," p. 103.

18. Lawrence, *Beowulf and Epic Tradition*, p. 22. Jeffrey Helterman, *"Beowulf:* The Archetype Enters History," *ELH*, xxv, no. 1 (March, 1968), pp. 1–20, does not answer my argument. *Additional Note.* The discovery, subsequent to original publication of my essay, that *Beowulf* incorporates the Celtic legend of *Suibne* attests the active role of Celtic missionaries in fostering early Anglian poetry. (See James Carney, "The Irish Elements in *Beowulf*," ch. III in his *Studies in Irish Literature and History*. Dublin, 1955.) Since the Celtic Rite retained old liturgical forms longer than the Latin Rite, it is the more likely that the fullness of parallel between Beowulf's encounter with Grendel's mother and the Office of Baptism in its antique form reflects both a conscious poetic intention and a continued use of the older ceremonial in the Hiberno-Saxon church.

11. JOSEPH OF ARIMATHEA AND A CHALICE

1. Jessie L. Weston, *From Ritual to Romance* (Garden City, N.Y.: Doubleday and Co., 1957; originally published in 1920), p. 2. Cf. the equally emphatic statement by J. Armitage Robinson, *Two Glastonbury Legends* (Cambridge: Cambridge University Press, 1926), p. 39: "the Holy Grail was purely an invention of the romances, and never at any time received ecclesiastical sanction."

2. Weston, *From Ritual*, p. 70, n. 3.

3. Robert de Boron (late 12th c.), *Le roman de l'estoire dou Graal*, ed. William A. Nitze (Paris: Honoré Champion, 1927), pp. xl, 124. See also Nitze, "Messire Robert de Boron: Enquiry and Summary," *Speculum*, 28 (April, 1953): 283f. In his edition of Boron's *Roman*, Nitze acknowledged that the relationship between Honorius and the Grail legend had already been noted by Adolf Birch-Hirschfeld, *Die Sage vom Gral* (Leipzig, 1877), p. 217.

4. End of the Canon of the Mass just before the Lord's Prayer.

5. Honorius Augustodunensis (mid-12th c.), *Gemma animae*, I, 47 (Migne, PL, clxxii, 558BC). On Honorius, see M.

Manitius, *Geschichte der lateinischen Literatur des Mittelalters* (Munich: Beck, 1931), 3: 364–76.

6. Pierre le Gentil, "The Work of Robert de Boron and the Didot Perceval," in *Arthurian Literature in the Middle Ages*, ed. R. S. Loomis (Oxford: Clarendon, 1959), p. 254.

7. Helen Adolf, *Visio Pacis: Holy City and Grail* (State College, Pa.: Pennsylvania State University Press, 1960), p. 13.

8. Ibid., p. 180.

9. Rupertus Tuitiensis (early 12th c.), *De divinis officiis*, II, 15 (PL, clxx, 45BC). On Rupert, see Manitius, *Geschichte*, pp. 127–35; or more briefly, G. E. McCracken and Allen Cabaniss, *Early Medieval Theology*, Library of Christian Classics, IX (Philadelphia: Westminster Press, 1957), pp. 249–56.

10. Allen Cabaniss, *Amalarius of Metz* (Amsterdam: North-Holland Publishing Co., 1954), *passim*. The assertion by Louis C. Gatto, "The Blood Theology of Medieval English Literature," *Studies in Medieval Culture*, 2 (1966), p. 90, that a legend of Joseph and containers of blood "can be traced as far back as the time of Isidore of Seville" is unfounded.

11. Luke 23:50–53.

12. Bede, *In Lucam evangelium expositio*, vi, 23 (PL, xcii, 621A); also in J. A. Giles, *Venerabilis Bedae opera quae supersunt omnia* (London: Whittaker and Co., 1844), 11: 371.

13. John 19:39f.

14. John 20:6f.; cited inaccurately in J. M. Hanssens, *Amalarii episcopi opera liturgica omnia* (*Studi e Testi*, 139; Città del Vaticano: Biblioteca Apostolica Vaticana, 1948), 2: 347.

15. A quotation from the Canon, not from Scripture.

16. Amalarius, *Liber officialis*, III, 26, 7–9 (Hanssens, *Amalarii*, pp. 345f.). Interestingly enough the name of Joseph of Arimathea is not listed in the Index of this fine modern edition.

17. Cabaniss, *Amalarius of Metz*, p. 100.

18. Ibid.

19. Seventh paragraph of the Canon.

20. Amalarius, *Liber officialis*, IV, 47, 1f. (Hanssens, *Amalarii*, p. 542).

21. One may cite, for instance, the late thirteenth century work of William Durand, bishop of Mende, *Rationale divinorum*

officiorum, ed. Joseph Dura (Naples: J. Dura, 1859), 4: 22, 23 (*ed. cit.*, p. 287f.):

"Thereupon the deacon approaches and for a moment lifts the sacrifice (the chalice with the corporal) from the altar; then just like the priest himself puts it down, because (as it is reported in John 20) Joseph of Arimathea and Nicodemus came and begging the body of Jesus from Pilate took it down and buried it. The priest therefore as he elevates represents Nicodemus; the elevation itself indicated Christ's deposition from the cross; the replacing [on the altar] indicates the placing in the sepulcher....

"It is fitting therefore while these words [*Praeceptis salutaribus moniti*] are being said that the body and blood should be lifted up and put down representing the lifting of Christ's body from the earth and its being placed in the sepulcher, because Joseph (who took it down from the cross, lifted it up from the earth, and placed it in the sepulcher) had been 'admonished' and taught by Christ's 'salutary commands,' as his faithful disciples had been. It is therefore said of him in Mark [15:43]: 'He too was looking for the kingdom of God.' The consecrated body and blood are lifted up at the same time, because Joseph himself (as certain ones say) placed the body with the blood together in the sepulcher....

"The deacon therefore puts the corporal over the mouth of the chalice when he sets it down, because when the Lord had been buried Nicodemus 'rolled a great stone at the door of the tomb' [Matthew 27:60]. The deacon also wrapping the chalice with the corporal represents Joseph, who 'wrapped' the Lord's body 'in a clean shroud' [Matt. 27:59]."

The significant words are the parenthetic ones, "as certain ones say" *(ut quidam ferunt)*. They suggest that, by the time of William Durand, Grail literature was in its turn affecting interpretation of the Liturgy. The name of Joseph of Arimathea does not appear in the Index of this edition of the *Rationale*.

Since reference is often made to Helinand (early 13th c.), *Chronicon*, XLV, *anno* 718 (PL, ccxii, 814D–815A), it is here included although it adds nothing for our particular purpose:

"A marvelous vision was revealed at that time to a certain hermit in Britain. It was about Saint Joseph the councillor who took the Lord's body down from the cross and about that bowl or dish in which the Lord ate with His disciples. A story entitled, 'Concerning the Grail,' was related about it by the same hermit. *Gradalis,* or in French *gradale,* is said to be a dish broad and somewhat deep, in which costly delicacies in their proper succession are usually served step by step [*gradatim*] by rich people, one morsel after another in different orders. In the vernacular language it is called *graalz* because it is pleasing [*grata*] and delightful to the one eating from it. This may be either because of the container, since it was perhaps of silver or some other precious metal; or because of its contents, that is, the manifold order of costly delicacies. I have not been able to find this story written in Latin. It is held by certain noblemen to be written only in French, but (as they say) it cannot be easily found in its entirety. I have not yet been able to secure this from anyone to read it carefully. But as soon as I can, I will translate the more truthful and useful parts succinctly into Latin."

The words translated above as "bowl" *(catinus)* and "dish" *(paropsis)* are the words employed respectively in the Vulgate, Mark 14:20 and Matthew 26:23, to render the Greek *trublion.* Reference is obviously to the Passover dish of charoseth (crushed fruits and bitter herbs), as appears by the mention of "delicacies" in it, not to the dish containing the matzoth or the one with the Paschal lamb.

22. See Cabaniss, *Amalarius of Metz,* pp. 44, 53, 64, etc., for other imaginative and original elements in the thought of Amalarius. I should perhaps add that while I agree in general with Urban T. Holmes and Amelia Klenke, *Chrétien, Troyes, and the Grail* (Chapel Hill: University of North Carolina Press, 1959), their book does not assist my argument.

12. ALLELUIA: A WORD AND ITS EFFECT

1. A well-known passage from the Annals of Xanten for the year 852; Reinhold Rau, ed., *Fontes ad historiam regni Francorum aevi Karolini illustrandam* (Berlin: Rutten und Loening, n. d., but *ca.* 1958), 2: 350.

2. Summarized from Notker, *Liber sequentiarum, praef.;* PL, cxxi, 1003C–1004C.

3. F. Brittain, *The Medieval Latin and Romance Lyric to* A.D. *1300*, 2nd ed. (Cambridge: Cambridge University Press, 1951), pp. 10–20.

4. Notker is viewed, in the light of current scholarship, as advancing (not inventing) the Sequence.

5. The so-called Alleluiatic Psalms are 104–106, 111–113, 115–117, 135, 146–150 (according to the Revised Standard Version enumeration).

6. Cited as in Revised Standard Version, except substitution of the spelling "Alleluia" for "Hallelujah."

7. Cited as translated by Moses Hadas, *The Third and Fourth Books of Maccabees* (New York: Harper and Bros. for the Dropsie College for Hebrew and Cognate Learning, 1953), p. 83, except again "Alleluia" instead of "Hallelujah."

8. Revelation 19:1, 3, 4, 6. In verses 1 and 6 Alleluia is part of a song; in verse 3 it is a shout of victory; and in verse 4 it is associated with another Hebrew word, the "Amen."

9. Tertullian, *De oratione*, 27; PL, i, 1301B.

10. Eric Werner, *The Sacred Bridge* (New York: Columbia University Press, 1959), pp. 155–68.

11. Ibid., p. 303.

12. Bede, *Historia ecclesiastica*, 1: 20; *Baedae Historia ecclesiastica gentis Anglorum*, ed. and trans. J. E. King (Loeb Classical Library; G. P. Putnam's Sons, 1930), 1: 92.

13. Sidonius, *Letters*, II, 10, 4; Sidonius, *Poems and Letters*, trans. W. B. Anderson (Loeb Classical Library; Cambridge, Mass.: Harvard University Press, 1936), 1: 466.

14. Bede, *Historia*, 2: 1; *Baedae Historia*, p. 196.

15. Bede, *Historia*, 2: 1; *Baedae Historia*, p. 202.

16. Bede, *Historia*, 2: 25; *Baedae Historia*, p. 112.

17. Amalarius, *Liber officialis*, III, 16, 3; J. M. Hanssens, *Amalarii episcopi opera liturgica omnia*, II (*Studi e Testi*, 139; Città del Vaticano: Biblioteca Apostolica Vaticana, 1948), p. 304.

18. Amalarius, *Liber officialis*, III, 13; Hanssens, *Amalarii*, 2: 301.

19. Amalarius, *Liber officialis*, I, 1, 16ff.; Hanssens, *Amalarii*, 2: 32ff.

20. Amalarius, *Liber officialis*, I, 1, 16ff.

21. *The Anglican Breviary* (Mount Sinai, L. I., N. Y.: Frank Gavin Liturgical Foundation, 1955), p. 400.

22. F. Cabrol, "Alleluia, Acclamation liturgique," *Dictionnaire d'archéologie chrétienne et de liturgie*, vol. 1 (Paris: Letouzey et Ané, 1907), cols. 1229-1246, esp. cols. 1241, 1245; J. M. Neale, *Mediaeval Hymns and Sequences*, 2nd ed. (London: Joseph Masters, 1863), pp. 42, 182.

23. Ibid.

24. G. G. Coulton, *From St. Francis to Dante*, 2nd ed. (London: Duckworth and Co., 1908), pp. 21-37; Ernst Kantorowicz, *Frederick the Second 1194-1250*, trans. E. O. Lorimer (New York: Frederick Ungar, 1957), pp. 396-98.

25. See Werner, *Sacred Bridge*, p. 311, nn. 126, 129, 130; p. 312, nn. 131, 132, 133; p. 548, n. 93. Werner gives appropriate documentation.

26. Ibid., p. 301.

27. Ibid. Werner himself has added greatly to both historical and musicological knowledge of Alleluia. Cabrol's article, cited above in note 22, is a sound, scholarly presentation. Preceding Cabrol's treatment is P. Wagner's musicological essay, "Alleluia Chant," DACL, I, cols. 1226-1229.

13. SHAKESPEARE AND THE HOLY ROSARY

1. Cf. Allen Cabaniss, "A Note on the Liturgy of the Apocalypse," *Interpretation*, 7 (January, 1953), pp. 78-86, reprinted above, pp. 42-52; "The Harrowing of Hell, Psalm 24, and Pliny the Younger," *Vigiliae Christianae*, 7 (April, 1953), pp. 65-74, reprinted above, pp. 62-71; "A Footnote to the 'Petronian Question,'" *Classical Philology*, 49 (April, 1954), pp. 98-102, reprinted above, pp. 72-77; "A Note on the Date of the Great Advent Antiphons," *Speculum*, 23 (July, 1947), pp. 440-42, reprinted above, pp. 97-100; "*Beowulf* and the Liturgy," *Journal of English and Germanic Philology*, 54 (April, 1955), pp. 195-201, reprinted above, pp. 101-108.

2. The word *rose* appears in the sonnets thirteen times, as follows: I, line 2 (capitalized and italicized); XXXV, 2 (plural

and capitalized); LIV, 3, 6, 11 (capitalized, two plurals); LXVII, 8 (twice, capitalized, one plural); XCV, 2 (capitalized); XCVIII, 10 (capitalized); XCIX, 8 (plural and capitalized); CIX, 14 (capitalized); CXXX, 5f. (capitalized, plurals). For this paper I make use of the facsimile edition published by Columbia University Press for the Facsimile Text Society (New York, 1938), thereby assuming as substantially correct the original 1609 order of the Sonnets. Cf. Brents Stirling, *The Shakespeare Sonnet Order: Poems and Groups* (Berkeley: University of California Press, 1968), *passim.*

3. See the interesting discussion by R. J. Browne, "The Rosary in the *Nibelungenlied?*" *Germanic Review*, 30 (December, 1955), pp. 307–12.

4. Hyder E. Rollins, ed., *A New Variorum Edition of Shakespeare: The Sonnets*, i (Philadelphia: Lippincott, 1944), 21 n., citing Malone, ed. 1780.

5. Luke 1:48.

6. Luke 1:50.

7. Cf. the early fifteenth-century English carol "I syng of a mayden," as so penetratingly discussed by Leo Spitzer, "*Explication de Texte* Applied to Three Great Middle English Poems," *Archivum Linguisticum*, 3 (1951), fasc. II, pp. 152–64, esp. p. 156; reprinted in Spitzer, *Essays on English and American Literature*, ed. Anna Hatcher (Princeton: Princeton University Press, 1962), pp. 233–46.

8. Collect for the first Mass of Christmas: "Dominus, qui hanc sacratissiman noctem veri luminis fecisti illustratione clarescere: da, quaesumus, ut, cujus lucis mysteria in terra cognovimus, ejus quoque gaudiis in caelo perfruamur...."

9. Luke 2:35.

10. Matt. 26:36–44, and parallels.

11. Cf. Matt. 26:40, and parallels.

12. Cf. Ps. 106:16 (Vulgate) and many similar passages assembled and discussed in Cabaniss, "The Harrowing of Hell, Psalm 24, and Pliny the Younger" (see note 1 above). Leslie Hotson, *Shakespeare's Sonnets Dated and Other Essays* (London: Hart-Davis, 1949), pp. 4–21, has made some very interesting observations about this sonnet.

13. J. H. de Groot, *The Shakespeares and "The Old Faith"* (New York: King's Crown Press, 1946).

14. Ibid., p. 157; see also pp. 2, 224, for similar but briefer statements.

15. Ernest Hatch Wilkins, *The Invention of the Sonnet and Other Studies in Italian Literature* (Rome: Edizioni di Storia e Letteratura., 1959).

16. Cf., *inter alia*, Houston Peterson, ed., *The Book of Sonnet Sequences* (New York: Longmans, Green and Co., 1929), p. viii: "Sequences of sonnets developed in Italy in the thirteenth century almost as early as the sonnet itself."

17. The great collection, *Analecta hymnica medii aevi*, by G. M. Dreves, C. Blume, and H. M. Bannister, has in its 55 volumes (Leipzig, 1886–1922), many of the *psalteria*, showing an almost geometrical multiplicity of variations.

18. It is possible also that there may exist an inner and more profound relation between the sonnet form and the liturgical prayer called the *collect*. Clarity, precision, fixity, economy, and unity characterize both. But an investigation of this possibility would require another paper.

19. See, e. g., Paul Lehmann, *Parodistische Texte* (Munich: Drei Masken Verlag, 1923), edited to illustrate his slightly earlier *Die Parodie im Mittelalter*.

20. T. F. Simmons, ed., *The Lay Folks Mass Book*, EETS, Original series, No. 71 (London: N. Trubner and Co., 1879).

21. The important work on the history of the Rosary is a part of a series of articles by Herbert Thurston on "Our Popular Devotions." He deals specifically with the Rosary in *The Month*, 96 (1900): no. 436 (October), pp. 403–18; no. 437 (November), pp. 513–27; no. 438 (December), pp. 620–37; 97 (1901): no. 439 (January), pp. 67–79; no. 440 (February), pp. 172–88; no. 441 (March), pp. 286–304; no. 442 (April), pp. 383–404; see also "The Names of the Rosary," *The Month*, 103 (1908): pt. 1, no. 527 (May), pp. 518–29, and pt. 2, no. 528 (June), pp. 610–23; also "Genuflexions and Aves: A Study in Rosary Origins," *The Month*, 127 (1916): pt. 1, no. 623 (May), pp. 441–52, and pt. 2, no. 624 (June), pp. 546–59. Thurston has summarized his studies in the article, "Chapelet," in F. Cabrol

and H. Leclercq, eds., *Dictionnaire d'archéologie chrétienne et de liturgie*, vol. 3, cols. 399–406.

22. In addition to the citations in the preceding note, consult Thurston, "The Dedication of the Month of May to Our Lady," *The Month*, 97 (May, 1901), pp. 470–83; and "Notes on Familiar Prayers, I: The Origins of the Hail Mary," *The Month*, 121 (1913): no. 584 (February), pp. 162–76; no. 586 (April), pp. 379–84 (pp. 384–88 discuss the Regina Coeli).

23. Fifth lection of Matins for the feast of the Most Holy Rosary (Oct. 7): "ut Rosarium populis praedicare, *velut singulare adversus haereses* ac vitia *praesidium*. . . ." Italics mine.

24. *Novelas ejemplares, prologo al lector*, in Miguel de Cervantes Saavedra, *Obras Completas*, ed A. V. Prat (Madrid: Aguilar, 1952), p. 769.

25. Sixth lection of Matins for feast of the Most Holy Rosary.

26. John L. Motley, *The Rise of the Dutch Republic*, in *The Complete Works of John L. Motley* (New York: Kelmscott, 1900), 4: 263, 399.

27. Thurston, "The Rosary," *The Month*, 96 (December, 1900), p. 635; also "The so-called Bridgettine [*sic*] Rosary," *The Month*, 100 (August, 1902), pp. 189–203.

28. Queen Elizabeth I is reputed to have been as devout a user of the Rosary as her sister Mary had been.

EPILOGUE

1. Allen Cabaniss, "Eine Quelle zu Faulkners 'Die Fabel,' " *Schweizer Monatshefte* (Zürich), December, 1957, pp. 820–22 (kindly translated for me by Professor François Bucher); in slightly different form as, "A Source of Faulkner's *Fable*," *Studies in English*, 6 (1965), pp. 87–89.

2. I have offered new versions of the Apostles' and Nicene Creeds, *Gloria Patri*, and *Te Deum* in a paper, "Before it is Too Late," *Reformed Liturgics*, 5 (Spring, 1968), pp. 35–39.

Index

Adam, 104, 105, 107.
Adams, Henry (*Mont-Saint-Michel and Chartres*), 139.
Adolf, Helen (*Visio Pacis: Holy City and Grail*), 110, 165.
Aella, 118.
Agobard (*De Judaicis superstitionibus*), 156.
Alain de la Roche, 131.
Alcuin, 112.
Alexamenos, 94.
Alliluyeva, Svetlana, 134.
Amalarius (*Liber officialis*), 16, 110, 112, 113, 119, 138, 142, 146, 163, 165, 167, 168.
Anderson, G. K. (*The Literature of the Anglo-Saxons*), 163.
Anglican Breviary, The, 169.
Angus, S. (*The Mystery-Religions and Christianity*), 137.
Antoninus Pius, 13, 45, 50.
Apostolic Constitutions, 48, 145.
Auerbach, Erich (*Mimesis*), 138.

Augustine of Canterbury, 118.
Avvakum (*Life of the Archpriest Avvakum by Himself*), 134.

Baehrens, E. (*Poetae Latini minores*), 154.
Bagnani, Gilbert (*Arbiter of Elegance: A Study of the Life and Works of C. Petronius*), 157, 158.
Bannister, H. M., *see* Dreves, G. M.
Baptism, 15, 16, 25, 27, 29, 31, 32, 33, 44, 47, 48, 49, 50, 64, 103, 104, 105, 106, 107, 108, 143, 161, 162, 163.
Baudelaire, Charles ("Infernal Litanies"), 134.
Bäumer, Suitbert (*Histoire du Bréviaire*), 150.
Bede, the Venerable (*Historia ecclesiastica; In Lucam ... expositio*), 101, 111, 112, 118, 163, 165, 168.
Beowulf, 101–108, 122, 161–164, 169.
Berlioz, Hector, 134.

Birch-Hirschfeld, Adolf *(Die Sage vom Gral)*, 164.

Blume, C., *see* Dreves, G. M.

Boccaccio, Giovanni *(Decameron)*, 17.

Boethius *(De consolatione philosophiae)*, 99, 100, 122, 160, 161.

Boniface, 163.

Bonjour, Adrian ("Monsters Crouching and Critics Rampant"), 163.

Boron, Robert de, *see* Robert de Boron.

Bouyer, Louis *(The Paschal Mystery)*, 151, 162.

Brandon, S. G. F. *(The Fall of Jerusalem and the Christian Church)*, 154.

Breviarium Monasticum, 53, 146, 160.

Brewer, Raymond R. ("The Influence of Greek Drama on the Apocalypse of John"), 144.

Bright, J. W. ("The Relation of the Caedmonian *Exodus* to the Liturgy"), 108, 163, 164.

Brittain, F. *(The Medieval Latin and Romance Lyric to A. D. 1300)*, 168.

Brodeur, A. G. ("The Structure and Unity of *Beowulf*"), 163.

Browne, R. J. ("The Rosary in the *Nibelungenlied?*"), 170.

Bücheler, F. *(Petronii Satirae)*, 152.

Bucher, François, 172.

Bunyan, John *(Pilgrim's Progress)*, 134.

Burns, Robert, 134.

Burriss, E. E., 154.

Cabrol, F. ("L'avent liturgique"; "Avent"; "Alleluia, Acclamation liturgique"), 97, 98, 160, 169.

Caedmon *(Exodus)*, 107, 161.

Carney, James *(Studies in Irish Literature and History)*, 164.

Carrington, Philip *(The Primitive Christian Calendar; The Early Christian Church)*, 14, 55, 137, 142, 146, 157.

Case, Shirley J. *(Experience with the Supernatural in Early Christianity)*, 137.

Cervantes Saavedra, Miguel de *(Novelas ejemplares)*, 131, 172.

Celsus *(True Discourse)*, 94, 159.

Chambers, R. W. *(Beowulf: An Introduction)*, 161, 162.

Charlemagne, 108, 139, 163.

Chaucer, Geoffrey *(Canterbury Tales)*, 17.

Clark, Kenneth W. ("Worship in the Jerusalem after A. D. 70"), 136.

Clayton, F. W. ("Tacitus and Nero's Persecution of the Christians"), 155.

Clement of Rome *(Letter to the Corinthians)*, 46, 144.

Collignon, A. *(Étude sur Pétrone)*, 154.

Cornelius Fronto, M., 32.

Coulton, G. G. *(Medieval Panorama; From St. Francis to Dante)*, 43, 143, 169.

Cranmer, Thomas, 133.

Cross, F. L. *(1 Peter: A Paschal Liturgy)*, 15, 32, 137, 140.

Cullmann, Oscar *(Early Christian Worship/Le culte dans l'église primitive; The Early Church; Les sacrements dans l'évangile johannique)*, 139, 142, 148.

Cumont, F. *(Oriental Religions in Roman Paganism; Lux Perpetua)*, 137, 151.

Cynewulf *(Christ)*, 97, 107, 108.

Cyril of Jerusalem, 105.

Daniélou, Jean *(Bible et Liturgie)*, 136, 139, 142, 162.

de Groot, J. H., *see* Groot, J. H. de.

de Ruyt, F., *see* Ruyt, F. de.

Diekmann, G. L. *(The Easter Vigil Arranged for Use in Parishes)*, 142.

Dictionnaire d'archéologie chrétienne et de liturgie, ed. F. Cabrol and H. Leclercq, 98, 156, 169, 172.

Didache, 16, 27, 47, 144, 145.

Divine Office, the, 16, 36, 53, 54, 63, 117, 119, 124, 130, 133, 172.

Dix, Gregory *(The Shape of the Liturgy)*, 71, 146, 148, 151, 161.

Dominic the Prussian, 131.

Douglas, Winfred *(The Monastic Diurnal)*, 160.

Dreves, G. M., C. Blume, H. M. Bannister *(Analecta hymnica medii aevi)*, 171.

Duchesne, Louis *(Christian Worship)*, 146, 151, 161, 162.

Durand, William, *see* William Durand.

Egher, Henry, 131.

Eliot, T. S. *(Murder in the Cathedral)*, 134.

Elizabeth I, queen, 172.

Ennodius, 98.

Ermoldus Nigellus *(De rebus gestis Ludovici pii)*, 163.

Eucharist/Mass, 13, 16, 24, 25, 26, 27, 28, 29, 30, 31, 32, 33, 36, 40, 41, 44, 45, 46, 47, 48, 49, 50, 51, 52, 53, 99, 105, 106, 109, 110, 111, 112, 113, 115, 117, 119, 120, 121,

130, 133, 135, 139, 141, 143, 148, 165, 166, 170.

Eusebius *(Ecclesiastical History)*, 136.

Eve, 22, 28, 104.

Faulkner, William *(A Fable)*, 96, 134, 159, 160, 172.

Fisher, C. D. *(C. Taciti historiarum libri)*, 155.

Flavian, 82.

Florus of Lyons, 138.

Fortescue, Adrian (ed., Boethius, *De consolatione philosophiae; The Ceremonies of the Roman Rite Described)*, 99, 160, 161.

France, Anatole *(Thais)*, 134.

Francis of Assisi, 24.

Franz, Adolf *(Die Messe im deutschen Mittelalter)*, 138.

Freehof, Solomon B. *(The Book of Psalms: A Commentary)*, 150.

Frois, Bernard Le, *see* LeFrois, Bernard

Fry, Christopher *(A Phoenix too Frequent)*, 81.

Fulgentius, 98.

Gang, T. M. ("Approaches to *Beowulf*"), 163.

Gaster, T. H. *(Festivals of the Jewish Year)*, 136, 142.

Gatto, Louis C. ("The Blood Theology of Medieval English Literature"), 165.

Gesta Romanorum, 17.

Gentil, Pierre le, *see* le Gentil, Pierre.

Germanus of Auxerre, 117.

Giles, J. A. *(Venerabilis Bedae opera)*, 165.

Girvan, Ritchie *(Beowulf and the Seventh Century)*, 161.

Goethe, J. W. von, 134.

Goodspeed, E. J. *(The Meaning of Ephesians)*, 137.

Grant, R. M. ("Pliny and the Christians"), 151.

Gregory the Great, 98, 99, 100, 118.

Grendel, 101, 102, 103.

Grisebach, Eduard *(Die Wanderung der Novelle von der Treulosen Wittwe durch die Weltliteratur)*, 91, 158.

Groot, J. H. de *(The Shakespeares and "The Old Faith")*, 129, 171.

Guido of Arezzo, 114.

Guilding, Aileen *(The Fourth Gospel and Jewish Worship)*, 15, 137.

Gundry, Robert H. (" 'Verba Christi' in I Peter"), 140.

Hadas, Moses *(The Third and Fourth Books of Maccabees)*, 168.

Handel, George Frederick, 63, 121.

Hanssens, J. M. *(Amalarii*

episcopi opera liturgica omnia), 146, 163, 165.

Hardison, O. B., Jr. (*Christian Rite and Christian Drama in the Middle Ages*), 17, 138.

Headlam, A. C., *see* Sanday, W.

Helinand (*Chronicon*), 166.

Helterman, Jeffrey ("*Beowulf:* The Archetype Enters History"), 164.

Hildebert of Tours, 110.

Hirn Yrjö (*The Sacred Shrine*), 138.

Holmes, Urban T., Jr., and Amelia Klenke (*Chrétien, Troyes, and the Grail*), 167.

Honorius of Autun (*Gemma animae*), 109, 110, 113, 164.

Hosius, Carl, *see* Schanz, Martin.

Hotson, Leslie (*Shakespeare's Sonnets Dated and Other Essays*), 170.

Hulme, W. H. (*The Middle-English Harrowing of Hell and Gospel of Nicodemus*), 149.

Huysmans, Joris-Karl (*La Cathédrale; L'Oblat; Là-Bas*), 134.

Ignatius of Antioch (*Romans; Smyrnaeans; Ephesians; Philadelphians; Magnesians; Trallians*), 13, 16, 26, 46, 47, 49, 55, 56, 57, 137, 139, 144, 145, 147.

Irenaeus (*Against Heresies*), 151.

Isidore of Seville, 165.

Iso, 115.

Jacobus da Varagine (*The Golden Legend*), 17.

James, M. R. (*The Apocryphal New Testament*), 147, 149, 153, 158, 161.

James, *Protevangelium* (or *Gospel*) *of*, 55, 159.

James the Just, 11.

Jeremias, Joachim (*The Lord's Prayer; The Eucharistic Words of Jesus*), 140, 141.

Jesse of Amiens (*De baptismo*), 163.

John of Austria, Don, 131, 132.

John of Salisbury (*Policraticus*), 82.

John the Baptist, 60.

John the Evangelist, 11.

Joseph of Arimathea, 58, 109–113, 138, 166.

Joseph of Nazareth, 58.

Josephus, Flavius (*Antiquities of the Jews*), 136.

Justin Martyr (*Apology; Dialogue with Trypho*), 13, 16, 40, 44, 45, 47, 48, 49, 50, 51, 52, 137, 143, 144, 145, 151.

Kalendar/Lectionary/Festivals, 15, 23, 24, 26, 28,

33, 35, 36, 51, 53, 54, 55, 57, 59, 60, 61, 68, 69, 71, 97, 103, 104, 105, 106, 107, 108, 119, 120, 123, 124, 125, 128, 131, 134, 136, 137, 138, 139, 140, 141, 142, 143, 144, 145, 146, 147, 148, 149, 150, 151, 153, 158, 160, 161, 162, 169, 170, 172.

Kantorowicz, Ernst H. *(Frederick the Second)*, 169.

Kennedy, C. W. *(The Earliest English Poetry)*, 163.

Klaeber, Fr. *(Beowulf and the Fight at Finnsburg;* "Die christlichen Elemente im Beowulf"), 101, 161.

Klenke, Amelia, *see* Holmes, Urban T., Jr.

Kroll, W., *see* Wissowa, Georg.

Lawrence, W. W. *(Beowulf and the Epic Tradition)*, 108, 161, 164.

Lay Folks Mass Book, 130.

Leclercq, H. ("Bithynie"), 156.

LeFrois, Bernard J. *(The Woman Clothed with the Sun)*, 146, 147, 148.

le Gentil, Pierre ("The Work of Robert de Boron and the Didot Perceval"), 110, 165.

Leidrad *(De sacramento baptismi; Epistola II)*, 163.

Lietzmann, Hans *(Die klementinische Liturgie)*, 145.

Liszt, Franz, 134.

Loomis, L. R. *(The Book of the Popes)*, 148.

Loomis, R. S. *(Arthurian Literature in the Middle Ages)*, 165.

Lord's Prayer, the, 15, 24, 25, 29, 33, 129, 140.

Lucian of Samosata *(Death of Peregrinus; The Runaways)*, 94, 95, 159.

Lytle, Andrew *(At the Moon's Inn)*, 134.

MacCulloch, J. A. *(The Harrowing of Hell)*, 149.

Maniet, A., 155.

Manitius, Max *(Geschichte der lateinischen Literatur des Mittelalters)*, 165.

Marcellus, 115.

Marcion, 75, 155.

Marcus Aurelius *(Eis heauton)*, 32, 140.

Marmorale, E. V. *(La Questione Petroniana)*, 152, 154, 156.

Martin, R. P. *(Carmen Christi)*, 151.

Mary, the Blessed Virgin, 56, 58, 106, 123, 124, 125, 127, 129, 139.

Mary Magdalene, 58, 152.

Mary, mother of Joseph, 58, 152.

Mary I, queen of England, 172.

Mary, queen of Scotland,
132.
McCracken, George E. and
Allen Cabaniss (Early
Medieval Theology), 165.
Melito of Sardis (Peri
Pascha), 138.
Milligan, G., see Moulton,
J. H.
Milton, John, 134.
Minucius Felix (Octavius),
32, 140.
Missale Romanum, 53, 142,
146, 161.
Motley, John L. (The Rise
of the Dutch Republic),
172.
Moulton, J. H. and
G. Milligan (The
Vocabulary of the New
Testament), 152.
Mowry, Lucetta ("Revelation
4–5 and Early Christian
Liturgical Usage"), 143,
145.
Mozart, Wolfgang A., 121.

Neale, John M. (Mediaeval
Hymns and Sequences),
169.
Nero, 75, 154, 155, 157.
Nicodemus, 31, 110, 111, 166.
Nicodemus, Gospel of, 62,
68, 70, 149, 161.
Nitze, William A. (ed.,
Robert de Boron, Le roman
de l'estoire dou Graal;
"Messire Robert de Boron:

Enquiry and Summary"),
109, 113, 164.
Nock, A. D. (Conversion),
143.
Notker Balbulus (Liber
sequentiarum), 114, 115,
167.

Ogle, M. B. ("Bible Text or
Liturgy?"), 160.
O'Neill, Eugene (The
Fountain), 134.
Origen (Contra Celsum), 112,
159.

Panthera, 95.
Pater, Walter (Marius the
Epicurean), 14, 137.
Paul, Acts of, 75, 153.
People's Anglican Missal, The,
146.
Pervigilium Veneris, 157.
Peter, Gospel of, 79, 158.
Peterson, Eric (The Angels
and the Liturgy), 137.
Peterson, Houston (The Book
of Sonnet Sequences), 171.
Petronius Arbiter (Satiricon),
72–96, 122, 152–160.
Petronius, Publius, 77, 78, 79.
Phaedrus (Fabulae Aesopiae),
75, 82, 83, 86, 87, 88, 89, 90,
92, 93, 94, 95, 155, 158, 159.
Philo (Life of Moses), 136.
Pike, Joseph B. (Frivolities
of Courtiers and Footprints
of Philosophers), 158.
Pilate, 76, 110, 111, 152, 166.
Pilate, Acts of, 62.

Piper, Otto A. ("The Apocalypse of John and the Liturgy of the Ancient Church"), 143, 145.
Pitra, J. B. F., 121.
Pliny the Younger (Letters), 32, 42, 45, 46, 47, 48, 50, 62–71, 122, 140, 143, 144, 145, 149–151, 156.
Postgate, J. P. (Phaedri fabulae Aesopiae), 155, 158, 159.

Rand, E. K., 99, 160.
Rau, Reinhold (Fontes as historiam regni Francorum ... illustrandam), 167.
Reese, Gustave (Music in the Middle Ages; Music in the Renaissance), 138.
Remusat, J. P. A. (Contes chinois), 91, 158.
Robert de Boron (Le roman de l'estoire dou Graal), 109, 113, 164.
Robinson, J. Armitage (Two Glastonbury Legends), 164.
Robinson, John A. T. ("Elijah, John, and Jesus: An Essay in Detection"), 149.
Rollins, Hyder E. (A New Variorum Edition of Shakespeare: The Sonnets), 170.
Rose, K. F. C. (The Date and Author of the Satyricon), 157.
Rupert of Deutz (De divinis officiis), 110, 165.

Ruyt, F. de., 155.

Sage, Evan T. (Petronius: The Satiricon), 154, 158, 159.
Salimbene, 120.
Sanday, W. and A. C. Headlam (A Critical and Exegetical Commentary on the Epistle to the Romans), 154.
Sandmel, Samuel, 148.
Schanz, Martin and Carl Hosius (Geschichte der römischen Literatur), 158.
Schonfield, Hugh J. (According to the Hebrews; The Passover Plot), 95, 156, 159.
Scott, Walter, 134.
Sedgwick, W. B. (Cena Trimalchionis), 152.
Shakespeare, William (Sonnets), 122–132.
Shepherd, Massey H., Jr. (The Paschal Liturgy and the Apocalypse), 140, 143.
Sibinga, J. Smit ("Une citation du Cantique dans la Secunda Petri"), 141.
Sidonius Apollinaris (Letters), 36, 118, 142, 168.
Simmons, T. F. (The Lay Folks Mass Book), 171.
Simon, Marcel (Verus Israel), 154.
Simson, Otto G. von (Sacred Fortress), 139.
Spitzer, Leo (Essays on English and American Literature), 170.

Sprenger, James (coauthor of *Malleus maleficarum*), 131.
Stirling, Brents *(The Shakespeare Sonnet Order)*, 170.
Stott, Wilfred ("A note on the word KYPIAKH in Rev. i. 10"), 144, 145.
Stout, S. E., 145, 150.
Strand K. A. ("Another Look at 'Lord's Day' in the Early Church and in Rev. i. 10"), 145.
Sulpicius Severus *(Historia sacra)*, 155.
Symons, Thomas *(Regularis Concordia)*, 162.

Tacitus, C. *(Annals)*, 76, 77, 154, 155, 156, 157.
Taylor, Jeremy *(Holy Living and Dying)*, 81, 82, 158.
Tertullian *(De oratione; Apologeticus; On Flight in Persecution)*, 32, 117, 140, 151, 168.
Thackeray, H. St. J. *(The Septuagint and Jewish Worship)*, 136, 141.
Thurston, Herbert ("The Great Advent Antiphons"; "Our Popular Devotions"; "Chapelet"; "Notes on Familiar Prayers"), 97, 98, 100, 160, 171, 172.
Todd, F. A. *(Some Ancient Novels)*, 154.
Toldoth Jeshu, 96.
Tolkien, J. R. R. ("Beowulf: The Monsters and the Critics"), 162.

Trajan, 16, 46, 69, 122.
Trimalchio, 79, 152.
Tryphaena, 73, 75, 79, 153.

Van Buren, A. W., 154, 156.
Vergil *(Aeneid)*, 84, 85, 88, 105, 162.
Vincent of Lérins, 52.

Wagner, P. ("Alleluia Chant"), 169.
Weinburger, W. (ed., Boethius, *Philosophiae consolatio*), 99, 160.
Werner, Eric *(The Sacred Bridge)*, 138, 168, 169.
Weston, Jessie L. *(From Ritual to Romance)*, 109, 164.
Whatmough, Joshua, 155, 156.
Wilkins, Ernest H. *(The Invention of the Sonnet and Other Studies in Italian Literature)*, 171.
William Durand *(Rationale divinorum officiorum)*, 165, 166.
Willibald *(Vita Bonifatii)*, 163.
Willoughby, H. R. *(Pagan Regeneration)*, 137.
Wissowa, Georg and Wilhelm Kroll *(Real-Encyclopädie der Classischen Altertums Wissenschaft)*, 158.

Young, Karl *(The Drama of the Medieval Church)*, 138.